SIGNS *of* SPIRIT

ABOUT THE AUTHOR

Roland Comtois is a clear-sighted spiritual medium, a compelling inspirational speaker, host of the podcast *The Wisdom Keepers* and the TV show *Soul Stories*, author of *Signs of Spirit, And Then There Was Heaven*, and *16 Minutes*, and coauthor of *365 Days of Angel Prayers*. For over forty years, Roland has reached many along his vocational path from physical to spiritual healing. He has worked as a geriatric nurse, Reiki Master, metaphysical teacher, and grief specialist. The healing modalities and messages that he shares nurture and balance mind, body, and soul. Roland's daily commitment is to help people find comfort in life in spite of overwhelming loss, to show how to move beyond grief, and to pass on the message that eternal love is genuine. He is the founder of the Living Beyond Life Conference, now in its eleventh year. Roland is in negotiations with several media outlets to showcase his signature Purple Papers.

THE PURPLE PAPERS
and the
STORIES BEHIND THEM

SIGNS
of
SPIRIT

*A Medium's Handwritten Proof
of Life Beyond Death*

ROLAND COMTOIS

Llewellyn Publications
Woodbury, Minnesota

First Edition
First Printing, 2019

Book design by Samantha Penn
Cover design by Shira Atakpu
Interior photos by Roland Comtois

Llewellyn Publications is a registered trademark of Llewellyn Worldwide Ltd.

Library of Congress Cataloging-in-Publication Data
Names: Comtois, Roland, author.
Title: Signs of spirit : the purple papers and the stories behind them a medium's handwritten proof of life beyond death / Roland Comtois.
Description: First edition. | Woodbury, Minnesota : Llewellyn Publications, 2019.
Identifiers: LCCN 2019016701 (print) | LCCN 2019020587 (ebook) | ISBN 9780738757568 (ebook) | ISBN 9780738757452 (alk. paper)
Subjects: LCSH: Spirit writings. | Channeling (Spiritualism) | Future life—Miscellanea.
Classification: LCC BF1301 (ebook) | LCC BF1301 .C693 2019 (print) | DDC 133.9/3—dc23
LC record available at https://lccn.loc.gov/2019016701

Llewellyn Publications
A Division of Llewellyn Worldwide Ltd.
2143 Wooddale Drive
Woodbury, MN 55125-2989
www.llewellyn.com

Printed in the United States of America

ALSO BY ROLAND COMTOIS

And Then There Was Heaven

16 Minutes

To the thousands of people whose lives have been touched by loss and grief, and to the thousands more who have searched for truth of love beyond and the continuity of the soul, I dedicate this book to you.

CONTENTS

ACKNOWLEDGMENTS

To Cindy Clarke, for years of unwavering belief in the Purple Papers and the stories they tell. To Carrie Butts, for your outstanding contribution to the entire process of putting this book together. To Diane Lupo, for your willingness to go the distance.

Purple Paper Team: Dawn Penta, Tina Botticelli, Diane Lupo, Steve Lupo, White Swan, Barbara Conetta, JoAnn Wolff, June Fagan, Tracy Mignone, Kathy St. Germain, Chip Cingari, Nancy Cingari, and Patricia Pepler. Thank you for your support and, moreover, your willingness to help every person who is in need at my events.

To Roy Kavanaugh, thank you for your years of encouragement, inspiration, and friendship.

To my many supporters, for your years of constant and faithful support of the mission at large, I thank you.

To Kaitlin Comtois, Tim Morvan, Mom, Lilli, and Mabel, I love you!

Thank you to Llewellyn Publications for the opportunity to tell the Purple Papers stories.

THE PURPLE PAPERS: THEIR STORIES AND MINE

Long before I could understand why, voices have marched through my thoughts, an energetic force that flowed in and out of my consciousness. Emotions from people who had passed on, people I never knew, have always moved through my innermost being. I have come to accept that these feelings or messages are a part of my existence.

Much of my life has been an exploration of an interconnection with the spiritual realm, especially with those who have left the physical world. It seems that the departed are in a place where the ability to send messages and love is limitless.

In my teenage years, conversations, and then private sessions, about departed loved ones evolved. I found myself feeling something, wonderful and oddly joyful, moving through my entire being during these sessions. I automatically began writing "bits and pieces" of messages on tiny pieces of paper. As I adjusted to this experience, I learned to trust that what I was hearing and feeling was distinctly separate from myself. I did not initiate the messages of love and hope. They surprisingly sprung out from me, creating a poignant image for those needing the message.

The sounds. The visions. The energy. The messages never ceased and always amazed me. The silent voice found its tone, and often in the strangest of places, messages would arrive. Over the years, the voices grew stronger and multiplied inside me. I could no longer contain the messages solely in my mind and heart. The storytelling needed to be transcribed. The words had to be brought forth from what seemed like a cavernous cocoon of chatter. Each story needed to be honored and revered for the healing and love it brought.

Some years ago, after I had spent much time communicating with the "other side," I sought spiritual support through prayer and meditation. I hoped to understand the enormity of and my responsibility to the energy and the messages. I was heard. Something happened. As I became transfixed by a calmness, a holy, serene voice entered my consciousness and said, "Just write on purple paper," and after a very short pause, "the story you hear."

I thought, *Purple? I like purple!* It's such a glorious, spirit-filled color. It implies, at least to me, being one with God (i.e., light, divinity, spirit). I sat there bewildered by the experience for a second or two, but I knew there was only one thing that I could do, and that was to step forward. As with many instances in life, we are unsure why certain things happen. I feel strongly that this was a synchronized twinkling of the right moment, a prayer answered, and a new beginning all at once.

The Purple Papers, eleven by seventeen inches in size, were birthed into my consciousness by a force greater than me. As I began transcribing, the words and the stories and the vision emerged. Some saw doodles and strange drawings. To me, these papers were sacred love letters, inspired notes, writings of lost love, ignitions of hope, and the possibility that the voice from beyond was real. To my amazement, some messages even offered an apology for wrongdoing or recalled dismay that one person caused another.

I was transformed by the papers in ways I can barely explain. To think I was given the charge of delivering such profound and healing messages. Once prayers and meditations were complete, each time I sat in front of a blank sheet of purple paper, words and names of departed loved ones began to find their way from my black permanent marker to the paper. Colors danced across my vision simply to enhance the message on the Purple Papers. Drawings of beds and hearts, hospitals and houses, rainbows and flowers anchored the scene that was being told to me. The manner in which these images appeared enthralled me as did every word that made the story complete. Messages that held no meaning to me personally somehow created a fortress of wonderment within me.

I looked at the messages with a greater empathy. The understanding of the oneness that exists among us grew deeper. If we truly love, then that love becomes the defining communicator itself, no matter what.

The Purple Papers give voice to those who exist elsewhere. The Purple Papers showcase human kindness, explore forgiveness, and remind us to love. When a father apologized to his daughter about how he passed away, or a son who died unexpectedly tells why, or a husband who left home never to return explains his story, the Purple Papers become a momentary player in the legacy of that one story. *Gratitude and reverence* is my mantra as each Purple Paper's story finds its way home ... to the rightful owner.

I wondered how many moments of forgiveness, kindness shared, and love experienced would come as I stood, again, in front of a large audience at Rhode Island's esteemed and premier Stadium Theatre in Woonsocket, Rhode Island. With Purple Papers in hand, I waited as the maroon velour curtains slowly lifted from the stage floor. I saw an audience of hundreds of people, all thirsty for words, for hope, but more so for peace about the loss of a loved one. All praying that they would be the first person to receive a spiritual gift ... a message. All wondering if they would be the recipient of a Purple Paper.

As a light shined through the darkened theater, a voice shuttered through me: "There's my mom. She's back there. You have a Purple Paper for her." I ran to the Purple Papers, closed my eyes, felt the energy, and knew there was one for her. I searched. My staff searched. It was there within the hundreds of Purple Papers I had brought with me. I had a feeling it was hers, and that feeling filled every part of me, as it does every time one Purple Paper is delivered. I trusted that feeling because it was pure and knowing. It's that same feeling you get when you're embracing your child or holding your friend's hand through a difficult moment. Something happens in those spaces, just as it does when a Purple Paper is finding its way to someone.

I stood near the edge of the stage and held up high above my head the Purple Paper for all to see. Though the woman was seated nearly in the last row and beyond my sight of vision, I yelled out, pointed to her, and said, "I've been waiting for you." She looked around with amazement, thinking I was talking to the person behind her. Though she wished for it, she never thought that she would encounter her son through the voice of a medium and one Purple Paper. My heart was fluttering too. All I wanted to do was help her through her grief and loss.

The paper was written years before with such concise language about a boat, the water, a heart attack, his girl, and the story of his passing that doubt of whom it was from simply evaporated into thin air. Each word had been translated by a language spoken from spirit to me, and then from me to someone eager to experience solace over the loss of a loved one. I jumped off the stage, ran to her, and showed her the message. Tears blackened her face from the mascara applied earlier in the day. She said quietly in my left ear, "I feel better right now." Though the Purple Paper was recorded years ago, the young man's message of his unexpected passing was finally delivered to the rightful owner, his mom. Like all the Purple Papers, they too, in time, will find where they belong.

Time moves on and life has changed since the first Purple Papers. Thousands of messages and papers have been delivered, slowly and methodically, often timely and poignant for the families in need. Messages inscribed on Purple Papers not only affect one person but become symbols of possibilities for the rest of the audience. From gallery-type mediumship events to live Facebook shows (and everywhere in between), the Purple Papers and their stories have created a reality that the love of someone who has passed away is more powerful than death itself. The papers have become a catalyst for those seeking support and those searching for healing.

I understood early on that there was more to the who and what, the where and why of life. That living, and living lovingly, was the true guide to any life experience. This knowledge bridges the ceaseless and boundless connection that exists between us, and that bond remains long after someone passes.

Gratitude envelops me. I often sit there with my eyes closed and the papers close to my heart, with the hope that they will find their loved ones and that the story of who and what, where and why continues. I guess it is quite simple. The Purple Papers and the stories behind them tell us that we live on.

This book and the Purple Papers are meant for those open to the possibility that life exists beyond the human breath. It is for those who are willing to journey toward peace and to search beyond the boundaries of physical life.

Signs of Spirit is a glimpse into the afterlife. A peephole into the messages that our loved ones want to tell us.

The reader who accepts the mantle of delving into the Purple Paper stories becomes part of the stories themselves. Within the confines of each word and story is the resemblance of every human life. Loss of a loved one, and the hope for continuity of that love, becomes the driving force in our lives.

This book takes the reader down the pathway of loss and past the avenue of grief into a heartfelt and gentle reminder that our loved ones remain a part of us.

People suggested for years that I tell the stories of the Purple Papers. Some people had sent their stories long before the revelation of this book. Then word got out that something amazing was happening ... the storytelling of the Purple Papers was about to be unveiled. Many said they wanted to tell their stories, to celebrate their loved ones with the world and to showcase that love is truly eternal. Born from the infinite understanding of love everlasting, here is a telling glimpse of the thousands of Purple Papers that have been written and the stories that live on behind them.

In the back of this book are several Purple Papers, because "I've been waiting for you."

God is in here.
Spirit is in here.
Love is in here.
And they are all one and the same.

Chapter 1

TJ'S STORY
BY ADELE HIGGINS

There was no mistaking that the Purple Paper was meant for my daughter. As Roland described the images he had drawn, I felt my heart seize and break all over again. I looked at the paper he was holding in his hands, then turned away, my hands trembling as I covered my face, tears unplugged and streaming in silent torrents down my face. The message was about my son TJ and the tragic accident that took his life way too soon. A stick figure of a man lying next to a pool, a lightning bolt above him to the left. The initials CPR, designating not a person but an action, were hovering over him. And then written boldly in the corner were the words "There was nothing you could do. It wasn't your fault. I love you."

My daughter, Kiera, TJ's sister, was there when the unthinkable happened. Born a year apart, TJ adored his sister from day one and they always had a very special bond. Often mistaken for twins and lifelong best friends, they were living close to one another in Florida where they both had gone to college. She had just spent the "the best day ever" with her brother and his girlfriend, Carol, at Universal Studios in Orlando, Florida, days after we all celebrated TJ's twenty-fifth birthday together at a lakeside cabin in Michigan. That night they were together with a few of their friends having a barbecue outside by the pool, and someone knocked a lamp over. TJ tried to grab it before it fell into the pool. He missed and fell in with it, making contact with the water just when the plugged-in lamp did. The light went out of our lives that night.

Kiera had tried to save her brother that night, performing CPR to no avail. She had blamed herself ever since. TJ wanted her to know there wasn't anything she could have done. She was not responsible for what happened, and he didn't want her to suffer anymore.

Roland continued sharing messages of love from TJ, pausing to smile at me. "He's OK. He's happy. The sun is shining all around him. There's so much love here."

I smiled through my grief, knowing on some level that TJ was still here with us. It had been a few years since he passed, but it seemed a lifetime. Kiera and I were desperate for messages from him, for confirmation that he was all right, for peace of mind that he was safe in that ethereal place we call heaven. I knew in my heart that if given the opportunity, TJ would get a message to us. Did we believe in spiritual communications before he died? I'm not sure, but we are confirmed believers now.

Giving up was never in TJ's DNA. He was born in the summertime, on July 16, 1982, a blond cherub who reached for the stars as soon as he could walk. A child model, he was a natural charmer who turned heads and captured hearts the moment he walked into a room. Life was fun for him, especially when he was outdoors. He loved everything about nature and would spend hours walking in the woods, playing on the beach, boating, swimming, and fishing in the summer, and snowboarding on snowy, the-steeper-the-better slopes in winter.

Sadly, the outdoors would become his undoing when he was frequently misdiagnosed and then belatedly diagnosed at the tender age of six with Lyme disease. The key to conquering Lyme disease and its far-reaching ill effects is to catch it early and treat it aggressively. If left to run its course, Lyme, life-altering in every stage, can progress from the mild flu-like symptoms and muscle aches early sufferers endure to chronic crippling fatigue, severe joint pain, heart arrhythmias, neurological problems, impaired memory, and other increasingly debilitating conditions. This disease goes undetected far too often, and in the case of young children like TJ, it can be especially diffi-cult to eradicate if it isn't medically dealt with right away.

I watched helplessly as my always happy, energetic, young son struggled to do the things he had so loved. He tired easily. His smiles faded as his body hurt more and more each day. He endured endless doctor visits, hastily pre-scribed, nausea-inducing medications, and steroids that made him even sicker as the medical community blindly tried to heal whatever was ailing him. It wasn't until TJ came down with Bell's palsy two years later, when he was in the third grade, that the doctors took my fears that he had Lyme dis-ease seriously. By then, he was so sick that he had to miss an entire year of school as he was hooked up to an IV that delivered the long overdue antibi-otics to his little body. While his health flagged, his spirit remained as strong as ever and he soldiered on. He couldn't wait to start living his carefree life again.

TJ would have health issues due to Lyme for the rest of his life, somehow managing to work through the crushing headaches and painful body aches that would plague him all too frequently. But the disease had taken its toll. While once he looked forward to school, his classes no longer held his atten-tion. His mind wandered, looking for a place that would soothe his soul and nurture his spirit. He found it in writing, an exercise that was much more than a passing passion for him. He had the heart of a poet and during his high school years, he declared that he wanted to be a writer.

His poetry, insightful and sensitive, seemed to emanate from someone much older and wiser than a boy of his age. To say that he was an old soul would be an understatement. He could read people, understand them on a level not readily apparent to others. He had depth beyond his years, and he had the unique ability to make everyone around him feel like they were the only person in the room.

And how he could make them laugh. He had a wonderful sense of humor. In retrospect I think his zest for life and fun is what got him through some of the challenges he would face as he moved into his teens and his young adult life.

He changed schools a lot as he tried to cope with the ever-increasing neu-rological symptoms of Lyme. He tried different medications and treatment therapies, choosing to go it on his own when they proved ineffective time and time again. His poems became a refuge for him, a safe haven from his painful Lyme-induced headaches, as did the time he spent with friends and family outdoors. He especially loved fishing with his grandfather, a sport they shared from the time he was a little boy, and he would often tell me that "Pops had his back." They were very close and would remain so even after he passed.

The first Purple Paper I ever received from Roland reaffirmed their eternal bond. I had first heard about the possibility of connecting with the other side through friends who gently suggested that I might find solace in talking with a medium. Roland was hosting an intimate session of just eighteen people at a Connecticut health and wellness center not far from where we lived, and I bought a ticket to see him. I didn't know what to expect.

Strangers united by loss, we sat around an L-shaped table, eyes and ears glued to the bespectacled man in front of the room. He introduced himself to us by saying that he was not a fortune-teller, he was just the messenger, blessed with an intuitive gift that enabled him to connect with spirit. He cautioned that he may not have a message for everyone in the room, but he would reveal every communication he received.

You could hear a pin drop in the room as he began to speak. I didn't dare breathe lest I miss some familiar word or sign that was meant for me. Roland went around the room comforting a grieving wife, daughter, friend with messages and memories that visibly touched hearts. Tissues were passed as tears flowed and stories were told. Then he stopped in front of me. "There's someone here who has a message for you. He's so handsome. He was pushing his way in front of the others. He wants to reach out and put his arms around you," said Roland, as he continued to relay what he was hearing. "He's telling me how it all happened. 'This stuff is so new but I'm OK,' he says. 'I'm sorry,' he says. 'I'm sorry.'

"Gary's here too," added Roland, "and he says he's watching out for him." Then Roland handed me a Purple Paper. "I believe this belongs to you."

The Purple Paper was dated May 7, 2010, three years after TJ had passed. Written on it were the words "Gary says he's fine—This stuff is so new, but I'm OK." The message was from my father, Gary, TJ's beloved grandfather, Pops. He was letting me know that they were together, like they once were on earth. TJ was not alone.

I was beside myself with relief and felt a surge of happiness similar to the emotions I'd had in the past when I would see the two of them, side by side, heading off to the lake or the beach with their fishing rods in hand so long ago. My Purple Paper was all the proof I needed to hold on to those magical memories.

I would receive another Purple Paper from Roland a month later. This time the message was from TJ himself and it was dated June 8, 2010. It read, "Tell my mom Happy Mother's Day, Happy Father's Day—well, Happy Day." In one corner Roland had drawn a blazing sun. In another were the words "I love you!" Roland said TJ was sending a message to his mother and his step-father, Rick.

Roland talked about it always being sunny and bright where TJ was. "He says Jean, Adele, and Gary are with him too." Jean and Adele are TJ's grandmothers. My parents were with my son! Roland came closer and looked me directly in the eyes. "He's at peace."

For a mother to know that her child is happy and at peace, whether here or in heaven, is one of the greatest gifts we could hope for. I remain grateful for the gift I was given that day. It has brought me immeasurable comfort as I deal with the ongoing pain of his loss.

Knowing how much TJ loved his family and treasured our time together, I was sure he had more to say. I was right.

The name "Rich" was written on the next Purple Paper Roland gave to me during another one of his Connecticut events. Rich is TJ's little brother, and Rich idolized him. The feeling was mutual. I remember TJ saying that the day Rich was born was the happiest day of his life. Despite their ten-year age difference, TJ would make a concerted effort to include Rich whenever he could, treating him like an equal, never leaving him out of activities they could do together, always making sure he was OK.

On that same Purple Paper, Roland had drawn a heart with the figure of a boy inside it and a sun, of course, shining brightly in the sky. Written there were the words "I walk with you by the water."

I nodded and smiled even as my heart ached. Our walks at the beach, in Connecticut and in Florida, were very special to us. We made a point of taking them whenever we could. It was our time together, a time when TJ's troubles would be trumped by the pure joy he felt from the simple things in life, the things that really mattered. TJ loved the water. It was one of the places he felt the freedom he aspired to and wrote about in one of his poems, "Dear Released."

Dear Released
Bless your wondering heart
May it gain the ability
To escape the churning seas
That you cast upon it
And someday find land
Worthy of holding true
To the tides that break upon it
And forever represent your
Unharnessed spirit

Images of our walks together morphed into memories of TJ and his sister, arm in arm, running down the beach and riding their boogie boards into the rolling surf. Then when Rich came along, the two became a trio of laughter and smiles. Those were the best days. The feelings we experienced there were the stuff of TJ's poem.

TJ's life wasn't always about laughter and good times. Bad choices had caused consequences difficult to weather and rifts that often seemed insurmountable. Missteps had shaken his confidence and sense of self. But when we were together, he would shrug off his troubles and remind us not to sweat the small stuff. He was the life of the party no matter where he went, loving his friends and family and living every day to its fullest, like it was his last. After I read the last line of his poem "There's a Thin Line," I think he knew that love and light would win out in the end.

There's a Thin Line

I walked upon the thin line that lay across the scape.
I came upon a thin man that hid within the shadow of his cape.
I asked, "Why do you hide out here and cover yourself so?"
He said to me from the hollows of his cape
As he slowly slipped out close,
"Does not a brilliant flower hang as a loathsome bud?
Does not a butterfly lie cocooned tight and snug?
Beauty is hidden and held within the walls of time,
Just as the shadows that make the hours hold me to this line.
The same shaded blades fall and paint my face with darkness,
Winged beauty that bursts inside the bud lies in this timeless
scape gently harnessed.
All of time has a proper motive in its mind and certain
moments for each of us to shine."

I keep pictures and framed memories of TJ around the fireplace in one of my favorite rooms in our house. It's a place I often go to remember the happiness and love we shared in life and to have those wordless heart-to-heaven conversations that will never cease.

Imagine my surprise when Roland handed me yet another Purple Paper when Rick, TJ's stepfather, and I just happened to sit in on a live radio show for which Roland was the guest speaker. We were sitting outside the control room, watching him from behind the glass partition as he answered phone calls from the program's broadcast audience. During the break, he came out to talk to us, bringing the paper with him. It was dated February 12, 2011.

"He knows about your shrine," said Roland, "and it makes him happy. He likes the cap. He's asking about Rich, Richie." Rich happened to be ill at the time with a sinus infection, and somehow I wasn't surprised that TJ knew that as well and was concerned about his little brother's health.

I looked at the paper to see Roland's drawing. There was the fireplace and the photos arranged just like they were in my house. "I know where you put my important stuff," the written words said. "Thanks for being proud."

"TJ sends you signs," Roland told us. "Look for them and know that he has sent them as a reminder that he is still with you. That he loves you and always will."

Kiera, Rich, Rick, and I find signs all the time almost at the very moment when we think or talk about TJ. Often we see them in sets of three or five, a sign for each one of us in our family. Sometimes they are in the form of pennies dated 1982, the year TJ was born. We see TJ license plates and TJ fish markets. We've heard people answer the phone and say "Hi TJ" just when we wished we could hear his voice. We see people wearing the cap TJ wore and t-shirts too, branded with Oregon Golf Club.

We saw a "Welcome home TJ" banner on a highway overpass right after Roland autographed our copy of *And Then There Was Heaven* at his book signing with a similar "he's home" message. Rich has no doubt that he saw TJ in the mirror on the night of his sixteenth birthday party at the club we still belong to, where TJ enjoyed many family parties.

And Rick and I know without question that TJ orchestrated our chance meeting with his former girlfriend, Carol, when we were visiting Rollins College in Florida not too long ago, where he, Kiera, and now Rich went to school. I was sitting alone outside in a sidewalk café. Rick had gone into a nearby shop just as the song *Somewhere Over the Rainbow* by the Hawaiian singer Israel "Iz" Kamakawiwoʻole started playing on the radio. That was one of TJ's favorites, and we had played it at his memorial service. Rick stopped at the memory and looked over at the young woman standing beside him in the shop who was also visibly entranced by the song. It was Carol, now married and a new mom. They walked out together to see me in the café before Carol got into her car and drove home. Her car was parked right next to where I sat; if Rick hadn't seen her in the shop, I certainly would have seen her when she returned to her car. We didn't need to question the "chance" co-incidences we had just experienced. We knew it was TJ bringing the people he loved together once again.

Before he died, we were all together when we celebrated his last birthday in a family cottage in Michigan doing all those things he loved to do when he was a child. We fished and hiked, picked wild blueberries and made pan-cakes. We swam in a lake so cold it energized us from head to toe. We made fires to warm us inside and out. We sailed and sunned and talked long into the night as the days flew by. When it was time to pack up and leave, a cloud of irrepressible sadness came over me. I started to cry and couldn't stop.

Rich tried his best to comfort me, assuring me that we would see TJ again in Florida in a few months. Not long after TJ and Carol drove away heading to Florida, I remembered that I had left my reading glasses in their car. We called them and they turned around happily and came back with my glasses. I hugged and kissed my son again as we said our second, final goodbye.

He turned twenty-five six days before he died, and he had his whole life ahead of him. He had met the girl of his dreams and was planning to ask her to be his wife. He had faced his demons, righted his wrongs, and taken responsibility for the adult role he was now assuming. He was clearheaded, confident, and enthusiastic about the future. And he couldn't wait to see what was ahead.

He wrote "Beautiful Creature" not long before he left us, immortalizing the blessings he realized at the end of his journey to this time and place.

Beautiful Creature
I'm a beautiful creature
I say this because I didn't always know—
I'm a beautiful creature

I say this because I didn't always show it—
I'm a beautiful creature
Because I found the five Ls of life—
(God) I have the power of love to guide me
(Family) I have the power of love behind me
(Friends) I have the power of love beside me
(Girlfriend) I have the power of love that won't lie to me
(Self) And now I have found the power of love inside me

Losing a child is perhaps the most difficult experience anyone can face. As mothers, we spend our lives unconditionally loving, guiding, helping, and protecting our children, giving them the resources and support they need to be safe and thrive. As a teacher, I spent my career teaching skills that were designed to help children succeed on their way to adulthood.

But TJ turned out to be the teacher, as he taught us the most important lessons of all. Carol told me that heaven needed a soldier and that's what TJ is doing now. A young man of incredible strength and perseverance no matter the obstacle, he soldiered on and showed us the true meaning of love and life. We know that he is showing us still.

Chapter 2

NO MORE BROKEN DOORS
BY TONI JEAN WALL

On December 17, 2015, the world I knew changed forever. I lost my only child, Jonathon, at age twenty-four to mental illness. Jonathon was a bright, loving, articulate son. Despite the loss of his father at the young age of ten, he persevered and found his way, and we, mother and son, truly became one. He liked car racing like many boys his age. That always made me nervous. My six-foot-six boy was called "the gentle teddy bear" by his high school principal. "Another two hundred like him would be great," he often said to me. He loved heavy metal rock music and studied at the Musicians Institute on Hollywood Boulevard in Southern California. There he befriended a famous drummer, who so eloquently called my Jonathon his "brother" in a special written tribute.

After the loss of our beloved dog, Jonathon and I had it in our hearts to get another one. One thousand three hundred and eighty-four miles away was another Peekapoo toy dog. Beau would grace our house with such love. He would follow Jonathon around the house, simply attached to his heart.

They were the best of friends. Even Beau was different after Jonathon passed away.

Less than a month after Jonathon's passing, in January 2016, I saw Roland for the first time. I was at one of his presentations seeking answers, as many of us do when our lives are turned upside down and shattered by a moment in time. A hush fell over the room when he walked in, engaging us from the start with the words "I have a young man here who committed suicide." He looked directly at me as he said them and continued speaking. "Your son told me to tell you, 'Don't blame yourself.'" My heart stopped, my breath caught in my throat, and I sat there transfixed.

That night I received my first of seven Purple Paper messages from Roland. It depicted a door and written across it three times was "I'm sorry, Mom." In the right upper corner it read, "Tell my mom that her boy is free."

Roland said, "You know the meaning of the door." I did relate to it. When my son had a bipolar episode, he'd break the doors, but he never did apologize. After Roland gave me that first Purple Paper, he asked for a blank one and began to draw. He drew wings and a heart, the exact representation of the tattoo that I had etched on my arm in Jonathan's memory. I left the presentation that night with such a feeling of peace.

In March of that same year, I attended a convention where Roland was speaking. I received my second Purple Paper message then. This one was dated March 23, 2016, and it read, "I'm sorry I never told you how bad I really felt. I'm sorry that I left things the way I did. I know I made you crazy. I finally found peace." On the left side it read, "The door with the hole. Walking in the room." I know my son was speaking to Roland. I haven't gone into his room since he passed, and the doorknob is missing. That is the hole he is speaking about.

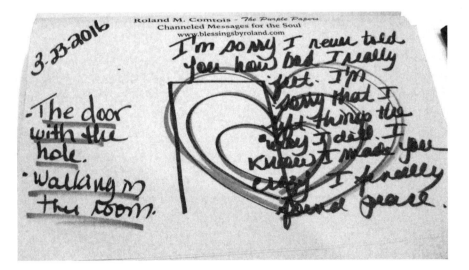

In May, I was blessed with my third Purple Paper message, dated May 3, 2016. It read: "Hey Mom, I tried to get healthy a few years before I passed. I wasn't mad at you. I was mad at my bipolar disease. We tried our best. Don't be afraid to open the door." Once again this message has so much meaning. When Jonathon had come home from college, he had lost a hundred pounds.

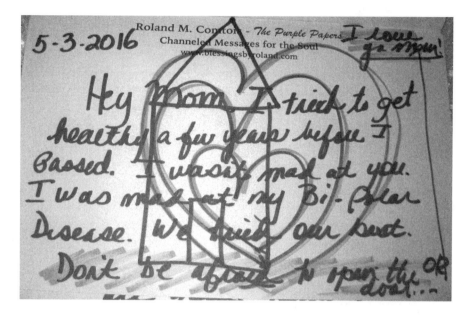

My next Purple Paper message, dated June 7, 2016, read, "I don't want to talk about my suicide anymore. I tried so hard to put things together for myself. I felt so lost (for a long time). You couldn't watch my every move. I saw the light, you know. It helped me find my way."

Roland M. Comtois - *The Purple Papers*
Channeled Messages for the Soul
www.blessingsbyroland.com

6-7-2016

I don't want to talk about my suicide anymore. I tried so hard to put things together for myself. I felt so lost (for a long time). You couldn't watch my every move. I saw light, you know. It helped me find my way.

My fifth Purple Paper was dated August 16, 2016. It read, "Johnny still has the 'best' sense of humor. I couldn't believe that it all ended like it did. But, I'm OK. Tell them more…"

Roland M. Comtois - *The Purple Papers*
Channeled Messages for the Soul
www.blessingsbyroland.com

8-16-2016

Johnny still has the "best" sense of humor. I couldn't believe that it all ended like it did. BUT, I'm OK. TELL THEM MORE…

My sixth Purple Paper message was dated September 12, 2016, and this one read, "Johnny says 'I'm free … I'm free. I know it was hard with me. Don't worry about me, OK? Look for the hearts!'"

The seventh read, "Hi Mom—I'm happy to know that Beau makes you feel better. I am there! I am there! You don't have to ask anymore. OK? I love you … I love you."

I feel so blessed to have received seven Purple Paper messages. They are all framed and hanging in my computer room. I often go in and read them and feel so at peace knowing my son is still with me. I miss my son more each day, but being blessed with my messages makes me know he is at peace.

8-11-2017   Roland M. Comtois   *The Purple Papers*
www.RolandComtois.net

Hi Mom—
I'm happy to know
that **Beau** makes you
feel better. I am there!
I am there! You don't have
to ask anymore. OK? I

love you...
I love you.

Chapter 3
ANGEL IN THE DRIVEWAY
BY JOANNE

Our dad passed very quickly and unexpectedly one bleak November day. He was the kindest, most unselfish person I have ever known. He was loving and generous and would do anything for anyone. His love for us was completely unconditional. Our grief at his passing was unbearable, and my sister and I found it beyond difficult to carry on without him.

While we dreaded spending the coming holidays with his empty seat at the table, the thought of him missing my children's graduations in the spring was especially difficult for me. My daughter was graduating from college the next May, and my son would receive his high school diploma a month later. What one would normally look forward to as a happy and eagerly awaited celebration of their individual achievements left me tearful and sad. All I could think of was how proud their grandfather would be to be a part of these special times in their lives and now he was gone. The mere idea of him not being there was unfathomable to me and I didn't know how I would get through it. To help alleviate the pain of his absence, I started to refer to my dad as our "angel." I would speak to him often and tell him that I knew he was looking down on his beloved grandchildren with love and pride from heaven. I told my children the same.

My mother was in ill health after my father passed and rarely left the house. So my sister and I would visit her daily, taking in her mail and newspapers and checking in on her. We were among her only visitors. One day as I was walking back to my car after visiting with her, I saw a little glimmer of something shiny in her driveway. I stopped to pick it up. It was a tiny little gold angel! That's when I knew without question that my dad was watching over us. Gazing up to the heavens, I thanked him for this very special gift and sign that he is indeed our angel and is always looking out for us. I carry it with me everywhere.

On June 14, 2011, my sister and I went to see Roland. We had heard about his spiritual gifts from friends and were hoping he would give us a message about Dad. We were sitting next to one another in a room full of people all hopeful for the same thing. Roland approached my sister first and said he needed to talk about our father. She held her breath.

Then he looked at me and said that there was an incredible energy between my sister and I and asked if we knew each other. Eyes wide, we looked at one another and then back at him. We responded that we were sisters. Roland immediately said that he had a Purple Paper for us and headed up to the front of the room to retrieve it.

It said, "My daughters need to know she's (they) got an angel up here now. You guys were so, so good to me."

I then showed Roland the tiny angel I had found in my mother's driveway. Thanks, Dad. You really are an angel.

Chapter 4

ORPHANED AT THIRTY-SEVEN
BY LINDA CHRISTENSEN

Orphaned at the age of thirty-seven, I lost my mom in March 2010, and then my sister passed in December 2011. When my dear friend, Erin, brought me to see Roland in Moodus, Connecticut, on September 22, 2012, we were the last two in the door and received the last seats in the front row. I had never heard of Roland until this invitation, and it was exciting to see the room packed full of people eager to hear what this man had to say about those who waited on the other side.

During the first half of the event, Roland looked at me with brief pauses as he paced up and down the aisle, speaking with other folks and evoking tears from some. Eventually, Roland stopped near where we were sitting and asked me who I was here for. I replied, "My whole family," as my voice cracked from having to repeat my response clearly and loudly.

Roland asked in disbelief, "How old are you, if you don't mind sharing?"

I replied, "Thirty-seven." Roland immediately asked that I stay after as there were a lot of messages coming through at once—imagine your family all fighting to be first in line! Erin looked over at me and quietly acknowledged her wish coming true. Before we arrived, Erin thoughtfully shared that she would be fine if Robert, her boyfriend who committed suicide a few months earlier, didn't come through as long as my family did. I asked Erin to stay with me afterward.

After folks had a chance to collect their Purple Papers and speak with Roland about their loved ones' messages, we all sat down together. Roland had a fresh tablet of purple paper with him and began to draw and number stick figures: Dad, my grandma, my sister, and Mom were drawn, but there were others present too, he said. My older sister, Vera, was the first to be channeled. Roland mentioned that she had decades of struggle; her message to me was, "I left with no closure or finishing." Roland shared a familiar smile as he said, "She's an interesting one," continuing to share her words about not having enough time to do her work here.

That actually brought me so much peace as Vera passed at age forty-two, after suffering from schizophrenia and chronic obstructive pulmonary disease. Her episodes began at the young age of eighteen. She battled ill health for over half her life. I always loved her. She resided at a secure care facility for her last five years, and being bedridden during her last days, she didn't get to say goodbye to her friends there. Serving as her conservator and only family member during the end of her life, I learned so much from Vera. Her memory and final gifts are forever treasured.

Roland continued writing on the same Purple Paper, "I'm sorry." He told me that this is my dad's apology: "I owe my daughter my love. I'm sorry for hurting you." To hear Roland share that my dad apologized for everything that wasn't settled led me to deep sobs and uncontrollable tears.

Roland began to channel another message: "A young man near you wants to say, 'Thank you, thank you!'" Roland turned to Erin while saying to me, "Thank you for taking care of her." Roland began to draw on a Purple Paper for Erin, channeling her late boyfriend, Robert.

Full of emotion, next was my mom's Purple Paper, written days earlier on September 14, 2012, which read, "My daughter really needs some peace. She keeps fighting about her decisions and the care. I am not unhappy with you. You have always done good stuff."

9-14-2012

Channeled Messages for the Soul
Roland M. Comtois
www.blessingsbyroland.com

My daughter really needs some peace. She keeps fighting about her decisions and the care. I am not unhappy with you. You have always done good stuff!

Mom had been diagnosed with stage 4 acute leukemia at Yale just days before. My mom's doctor called me after six that morning to share what a rough night she had and that mom wanted to see me again. Not an unusual request since we talked on the phone all the time. The doctor requested that I let her stabilize a few more hours before returning to the hospital. I arrived shortly after noon to see her and was surprised how much she had aged overnight and that she could only whisper short phrases. I had spent the previous afternoon with her and witnessed that she was virtually immobile on her own, having to nap from pure exhaustion after physical therapists came to sit her up in bed. When she woke, she said she didn't have any regrets, however, because she could sing in five languages. Her only regret was not learning how to speak one fluently! Ha! The care team and I agreed to begin hospice, and mom received her first dose of morphine. She then passed forty-five minutes later at 3 p.m.

Then there was the other Purple Paper, dated September 22, 2012, which showed an illustration of a clock face set at 3 o'clock and 3 p.m. scribed below it. The paper read, "It was past three am when I passed away. I just slept through it all. I am OK now. Remember how we would call each other all the time—I'll always love you!!"

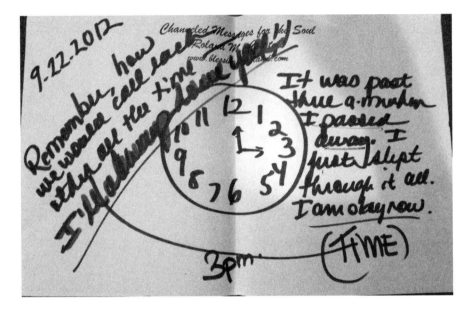

On another sheet, Roland drew a stick figure on a bed representing my mom and shared that everyone had to let her go, that she fought hard to hold everything together, and that she had no regret, but that she never got to live her full potential. She was mad at God for having to go so soon. "She loves you so much." In the same breath from Roland, Mom shared, "Thank you for holding me so close."

I was in complete awe of Roland at this point as he continued to speak about my father, that his life was just getting settled when he died, proclaiming that he "left you twice." He shared again that my mom has more peace now than in her entire life. Roland said she had a baby with her: "It's not a dog, but our dogs are fine." I think that baby may have symbolically been her first born, Vera. Roland assured me that my family would get me through this and that they were teachers for me. "You will teach, you will lead, you will guide." Roland finally asked, "Could you give yourself a break?"

This was a tremendous time in my life as both of my parents were only children (I had no extended family to grieve with). My parents divorced when I was four. I never saw my dad again after the age of eight when my mom moved us across the country to Connecticut. My dad passed in December 1994 during my senior year of college. Now forty-three, I have enjoyed a more peaceful life aware of my family's everlasting love.

I'm grateful for this gift of healing and love that is shared with so many. To my dear soul sister, Erin, thank you for sharing the path to discover that "love is eternal." Namaste.

Chapter 5

LOST NO MORE

BY BRUCE GALE

On January 31, 2014, I attended my first channeling event with Roland. I honestly had no expectations, but I must admit that I was secretly praying that I might be able to get some peace about my brother, Ed.

Edward Emerson Gale was my cool older brother. His behavior began to frighten all of us. One day Mom went into the cellar and found a large pile of rocks. She asked Ed if he had brought them in for any particular reason. With utter calm he told her of the "spirits" that inhabited them and gave him messages. When they put this together with other changes in his behavior, my parents became concerned for him. But it was when he was taken into custody by police for being found in camos with a loaded gun in a state forest that they became frightened about what those "messages" might be causing Ed to do that would be a danger to himself or to others.

He had a happy, normal childhood and was diagnosed with late onset of schizophrenia at the age of thirty-two. Although the impact of the disorder can often be eased by treatment, schizophrenia is a lifelong disorder that affects a person's ability to think, feel, and behave normatively. The key symptom that creates gravest concerns are the times of delusions or hallucinations the person deems real. People affected by this mental illness are often living in an alternative reality.

That was the first time we lost him.

When he was married and a new father, he became severely delusional and required psychotropic medication to function comfortably. With treatment, it is possible for people to live well with schizophrenia. Without it, the prognosis can be frightening. In my brother's case, a terrible misjudgment by his mental health clinician to lower medication dosage led to what could have been an avoidable tragedy. On Good Friday 1986, he took off in his car and we never saw him again. Ed now felt lost to us forever.

Now aware of how many thousands of families end up with missing persons due to mental health issues, my wife and mother helped form the National Network for the Missing and Homeless Mentally Ill in Massachusetts. Their mission was to try to locate persons with mental illnesses who are reported missing by families, loved ones, or friends and to reunite them when possible. Their work finding many missing persons for other families using data from other organizations and the shelter system across the nation had success, but not for our family. My brother Ed never interacted with the homeless or human services support systems. There were no records of his real name or Social Security number having been used after he disappeared. He did not turn up in homeless shelter records or prison system databases. No sign of him ever emerged in public records even to this day. Upon my mother's passing, we handed over our work to the National Alliance for the Mentally Ill (now the National Alliance on Mental Illness) so that the work would go forward by the next teams of caring family members.

The one thing I knew about him was that he had keen survival skills from his teen years. He would often retreat into a state forest and collect pieces of tree trunks in the family home basement before he left, so we thought he might have headed deep into some woods somewhere. That is how my wife and I would picture him as we prayed for him and worked with agencies to find him.

We longed for peace of mind about his well-being—or even of his demise. I had recently learned of the national network of medical examiners and police who were cataloguing DNA to identify all the deceased men and women who were never claimed by families and so existed as "Jane Doe" or

"John Doe" and I contacted them. This is the work of NamUs.gov. The ability to reunite families, even after their loved ones had passed, would bring great peace to so many. I then sought that peace that at least knowing whether he was alive or had passed would bring. My efforts here failed. No matches were recorded. It seemed as if my brother vanished forever.

And so the night I sat down in the room with other grieving souls to listen to Roland, I did open my heart as Roland asked. I opened my heart and spirit to any message for me. Not yet with belief it would come, but with hope.

Roland pointed to me and told me there was a man behind me. My father. I adored my father and was able to have wonderful times with him as we cared for him through his last years. I long felt him near me and now had affirmation that he "always was there." But when asked if he was whom I was hoping for, I was honestly able to say no.

Then I was uplifted as Roland went on to say that my mother was next to him! His description of them together fit truth only my wife and I in that room would know. I felt a wonderful calm love enfolding me.

But again, I was able to honestly and simply answer "no" when he asked if that was whom I was seeking.

Roland seemed content with those two responses, and we had a moment of comfortable silence as he listened and looked at me.

Then he said he saw a younger male with them—and that they said, "We got him." He repeated that several times. And it was exactly what my mother would say! It was an expression I recognized immediately.

This was a very comforting statement, but we also had another younger male family member that passed. I was not assuming who it was and simply took the joy of having Mom and Dad with me and whomever they were with. It was not a fully satisfying answer, but it brought me peace and I was grateful for any blessing of affirmation.

The event ended.

Before we left, Roland asked my wife to go up to him as he had "been waiting for her" and had to talk to her. She had held in her heart special prayers about the passing of her Native American grandmother, Gra, and her beloved niece and nephew, whom we had raised as our children and who passed as young adults. And she did, indeed, get messages from both.

Doe awoke one morning to a clear vision of her Gra at the foot of her bed with an arm around our "children"—all were younger, fully healthy, and shining with a gentle glow as they laughed in pure joy! Doe had been waiting for her Gra to make some contact, as she was raised and trained in tribal tradition. Gra's silence was bewildering. Once Gra showed up with the "children," she understood that Gra waited to bring them all together for reassurance!

I was so grateful for her sake and was gathering our coats to leave when I heard her cry out my name and beckon me forward.

As she was speaking with Roland, she had thanked him for the message voiced to me and mentioned that she felt it was about my brother. She talked about him having been missing these past decades and was compelled to mention his relationship with trees. His relationship with trees went back to our childhood and was a primary place where we bonded and shared stories—we went fishing, had long walks in the woods, and both felt a powerful, life-long relationship with trees. The Purple Paper revealed trees with a stream…just as it had been in our childhood forest where we spent countless hours fishing. This was affirmation, along with the words on the paper and Roland's spirit bringing him to speak to me that night.

Roland literally lit up in his countenance and began to go through his pile of Purple Papers. He pulled one out and read it and told me he had written it that morning as he prayed and was preparing for that night. It was dated that morning and had seven pine trees colored in with green. A stream, with blue lines, wound through the trees. And a figure was lying next to the stream. The words he had written that morning said, "I know you don't know what happened to me. All I know is that I'm in heaven. I saw 'the light' and followed it. I promise to stand with you, just you wait and see…all the signs will come."

Roland M. Comtois - *The Purple Papers*
Channeled Messages for the Soul
www.blessingsbyroland.com

1-31-2014

I know you don't know what happened to me. All I know is that I'm in heaven. I saw the light and followed it. I promise to stand with you. Just you wait and see --- all the signs will come.

"This," Roland said to me, "is for you."

My heart and spirit leapt as I could "hear" Ed's voice saying those words—in that cadence—with exactly that expression! "Just you wait and see ..."

I felt the peace that passes all understanding fill me, as I knew that Ed had used Roland's gift to grant me this time of healing and assurance.

Ed is lost no more!

Chapter 6

JAKE

BY CINDY CLARKE

There were only twenty of us there that night at Roland's signature Channeled Messages for the Soul event, each signing up weeks in advance for a more intimate opportunity to speak with him—and, hopefully, the loved ones we lost. Roland made it very clear that "before we get started, I am here to tell you that I am just the messenger. You don't need a guy like me to tell you what you can experience yourself. Your loved ones are right there beside you. They are always with you. Their love, your love, is eternal. The bonds between you and them can never be broken. I will share their messages with you and tell you what I see and hear," he explained. Then with a smile he added, "With the exception of your dogs. I don't do dogs."

We laughed, some heartily and others, like me, a bit tenuously and a little disappointed. I had just lost my fifteen-year-old chocolate Lab, Jake, an all-tongue and tail-wagging member of the family that brought endless joy to me, my daughters, and Butch, a huge cat that he had played and slept with for almost fifteen years.

We found Jake at our town's dog pound, where he was the sole occupant and was caged away from people in a cement box of a building that was located on the edge of the local dump. He was a purebred

Labrador, just eight and a half months old. He had been unceremoniously dumped there by someone who found his energy and exuberance to be way too much for his immaculate city apartment. A friend of the dog warden called me right after Jake was abandoned, knowing my love for furry, four-footed friends and my reluctance to ever say no to any living thing in need.

I was at the dog pound in an instant, peering in at the big brown puppy from a tiny speck of a window high up on the wall. As I looked in, he looked up…and bowed! He didn't have much room to dance but I think he would have given the space. It was obvious that he didn't like being away from the action or from anyone who would happen by. He had me the moment our eyes met.

Of course, I took him home with me that very afternoon. He bounded into the back of my red Chevy Blazer and was raring to go. The only sign of the trauma he experienced from being left behind by his person was an occasional whimper when we parked in our town center. Had he been there before with the person who didn't want him anymore?

Dogs are sensitive creatures. They have an uncanny sixth sense that lets them feel things others can't. They have the innate ability to detect unseen sadness, hurt, and heartbreak as if they were pieces of clothing displayed for the world to see. Jake came into our lives just when we needed him most. A divorce, a move, financial hardships, and an uncertain future had upended our family…and somehow this once-brokenhearted dog stepped up to the role of chief snuggler, face licker, and smile maker without hesitation.

He loved everyone he met: our family, who loved him unconditionally; the people he jumped on; to the baseball players who yelled at him when he caught an outfield ball; my girls' friends, who cringed at his wet tongue when they were all dressed up; and the once-wary dogs, cats, and rabbits he gently sniffed and made fast friends with. As often as he could be annoyingly "in your face," a day wasn't the same without him in it. He really was a joy.

Jake lived to a ripe old age for a big hundred-pound Lab, and I think he could have gone on a lot longer than his fifteen years simply on his will to love, despite his baseball-size cysts and swollen abdomen. No matter the ailment or the pain he would endure that last year of his life, he never let on that life was getting tough. He was still the same old playful Jake on the inside even as his body failed on the outside.

While walking had become increasingly difficult for him, one Saturday morning he couldn't get up. He was too heavy for me to lift, although I tried to fashion makeshift lifts and bands to help him stand. Nothing worked. Sunday passed the same way, with him lying on his bed, Butch by his side, tail thumping when he saw me, tongue outstretched to give me a loving lick. On the third day that Jake could not move, I called the vet for a home visit. His assessment left no hope for recovery. Jake would no longer be able to stand or walk, let alone run again.

It was time to let him go.

For days afterward, the emptiness in our house was palpable. With Jake gone, there was an eerie quiet in the front room where he slept and happily greeted visitors. Even his kitten Butch felt it, succumbing to his grief and passing away only six weeks later. I had never experienced anything like that before.

It may come as no surprise that Jake was on my mind when I sat there listening to Roland. What did happen that night was a surprise, though, and one no dog lover will ever forget.

7-18-2009

"Jake can RUN again"

Roland was immersed in the moment, sharing messages from moms, sisters, and best friends to sons, daughters, and brothers who ached to hear from them, when he stopped as though he was being nudged by someone— or some dog—that wanted his attention right then. He went over to where he had been sitting and pulled out a Purple Paper. He looked right at me as he read what he had written days earlier: "Jake can run again."

Chapter 7

THE FIRE

BY LIZZY

Five years younger than me, my little brother had just moved back home to Connecticut from Utah. Like so many of us who aren't sure of our path in life, he had been searching for himself, taking time off after high school to find his passion and purpose in life. He was a ski instructor who thrilled at the rush of accomplishment and freedom that skiing offered. But conquering the mountain slopes was more than a rite of passage for him. It was a metaphor that helped him build the confidence he needed to achieve his dream and reach the goals he set for himself.

He came home on top of the world, determined to go back to school and take his life in a new direction. He took two jobs, working in a restaurant and at a rock climbing gym, where he could still indulge his interests in adventure sports. He found a nice apartment he could afford in a multifamily house not far from his jobs, and life was good. He also wanted to go to college, and we had been working on his application together so he could be admitted to the upcoming semester, only a few months away.

That fall, in the wee hours of the morning, everything changed when his life, literally, went up in smoke.

There was a fire at his house that enflamed the entire structure. My brother had been asleep when the fire broke out but woke up to the unmistakable smell of smoke. In an attempt to make his escape from the house and the thickening, blinding smoke that clouded his way, he found himself in the bathroom instead of the door to the outside, which was actually right next to it. He must have been disoriented, but he had the presence of mind to cover his face with a wet washcloth while he waited for the firemen to rescue him.

That never happened. His body was found that afternoon, blocking the bathroom door from the other side.

When we learned about the fire and how my brother died, we were devastated. We couldn't imagine the terror and pain he must have felt. It was horrifying to even think about, and our grief multiplied.

A few years after he had passed, I had the opportunity to see Roland at an event in Stamford, Connecticut. I went with a friend who thought I might get some closure and comfort through Roland. She was right.

Roland told me that my brother sought safety in a bathroom during a fire but the firemen didn't know he was there. He was having a hard time breathing. Roland started to draw what he saw on a Purple Paper, outlining a house, a little room inside with no windows, flames coming off the roof, and stick figures of firemen all around. My brother wanted me to know that he was OK and at peace. "He couldn't move. It all happened so quickly. He is in a good place now," said Roland.

I got goose bumps as I listened to Roland tell my brother's story. The firemen had confirmed all of this after the fire, telling us that my brother had been trying to save himself and was waiting for help.

Roland continued with more messages. He told me my grandmother had come to get my brother that night and they were together now. "Your brother's with me," she said through Roland. That meant the world to me. Growing up, my grandmother and I used to take early morning walks out in the woods. She believed in garden fairies and the like and we would spend many happy hours looking for them. I smiled through my tears, amazed at how Roland even took on my grandmother's mannerisms as he was channeling her.

I thanked Roland for the gifts he gave me that night and stood up to go. As I was leaving, he called out to me and said, "Look for the butterflies." They would be sent to me from my loved ones in heaven to let me know that I was where I was supposed to be.

At the time I had seen Roland, I had been struggling with relationship issues. I had recently broken off a long-term relationship and a new one with someone equally wrong for me. I was ready to give up. A few weeks later, I met Mark, the man whom I would marry.

I can't help but think that my brother was behind our meeting, handpicking the person I was meant to share my life with. He and Mark had worked together at the restaurant and had become friendly before my brother died. It's amazing how miracles work.

And those butterflies Roland told me to look for? They came to me during a walk with friends not long after I met Mark. My friends had gone on ahead of me as we hiked along a trail near a popular pond. Lagging behind, I was just passing the bushes they had gone by when a flock of monarch butterflies fluttered in front of me and took off for the sky. Right then and there, I knew in my heart that I was on the right path after all, and that Mark was the one for me. We got married two years later.

I know my brother is always looking out for me. I still find monarch butterflies in the most unexpected places at the times I need them most and even had one land right on my finger.

I also received another sign as I was considering sharing my Purple Paper story in this book. I wanted to participate but couldn't find my Purple Paper anywhere. I worried that without it, my brother's story would not be told.

Several years ago I was filmed with Roland and the Purple Paper he had given to me for a television show. The producer had used a still photograph of that interview for a Facebook page about the show and even though the project was long over, there it was, some eight years later, in view as the featured photo on that page. We found that Purple Paper photo days before this book was due to the publisher. Coincidence? I think not.

Though I do not have the Purple Paper in my hand, I found solace in learning my brother's story still could be told. I went downstairs after receiving the phone call from the editor and noticed my brother's photo had slipped off the table where I kept it. I went to pick it up just as the station I had been listening to was playing "Somewhere Over the Rainbow" by the Hawaiian singer Israel "Iz" Kamakawiwoʻole. That was the very same song we played at my brother's funeral more than seventeen years before.

This story is for you, little brother. I am so happy you are still in my life.

Chapter 8

LETTERS FROM HEAVEN

BY CECELIA HENDER

I had never heard of Purple Papers. I had never even heard of Roland Comtois.

Then my husband died. His name was Stephen Michael Hender and he was the love of my life. Stephen died on March 23, 2011. That's when I know he went to heaven. The date on his gravestone says March 30, 2011, the day his body was found.

Stephen was a wonderful man. In the thirty-six years we were married, I never heard him say a bad thing about anyone. Really. He was always kind, and as I always said, he was a gentleman and a gentle man. He loved to garden and loved helping people. I loved to make him laugh. He always looked forward to retiring one day. "You and me, babe," he would say. But he was a very brittle diabetic and that was how he died.

He left for work one morning, looking as handsome as he always did. He was tall and slim and always looked like he walked out of a magazine. Dressed in his suit and tie, he left for work. I never saw him again.

When the normal time for Stephen to come home came and went and he didn't come home, I became worried. I realized he had not called me that day. I knew it was very busy and stressful at work, so at first I didn't think too much of it, until I was unable to reach him on the phone. I need to tell you that Stephen and I shared one

47

heart and one soul. You never saw one of us without the other, and we spoke often through the day. This was a particularly hard time for him at work, and I just figured it was busy. But when I was unable to reach him and my calls went directly into voice mail over and over, I knew something was wrong. I called my son Jeff to come. With the traffic, I thought it would take him about two hours to get to me.

I was standing at my kitchen counter, calling person after person that he worked with—I even called his bosses, who were no help at all. No one seemed at all concerned. I was frantic. It was then that I felt this pull in my chest—it seemed to go up from my chest and out the top of my head. I remember grabbing hold of the kitchen counter and the first thought that came to mind was that my soul left.

Stephen never came home that night. When Jeff arrived, we called the police immediately. We decided we needed help. I had already called all the hospitals to no avail and asked everyone I knew to pray. We sat on the couch, dozing off here and there and waited. I screamed in anguish out the front door. It was a snowy March night and I was worried if he was cold. Where could he be?

So many police came in and out of the house; there was so much anguish and endless questions. We were trying to fit this puzzle together. But I knew it was Wednesday and his pump would need to be changed for his insulin. Before he received the pump, he would give himself many shots of insulin daily, as well as testing his blood sugar many times a day. But with all the stress of the job issues this week, he wasn't testing as often, and he wasn't eating right during the day. I was fearful that his insulin levels were not right.

We spent a tortuous week praying and begging that he be found alive. He had come home many times with low blood sugar. I could tell by looking at him. I was always able to get his sugar back into range, even when he was "basically out of it" from low blood sugar. I begged God to give me this chance one more time. Let him be found so I can fix him again.

It took a week before they found his car. It was parked at the pond. We called it the Swan Pond because we used to watch the swans there. Some friends called us "the Swans" because swans mate for life. You never saw me without Stephen or Stephen without me. Now he was without me and I was without him. His car was found but he was nowhere in sight. The police and rescue squads searched the water—twice—and told me he was not in the pond. I was so glad! At least we had a shot of finding him, I thought, grabbing on to the slightest possibility of hope. But then, they went back in the pond one more time and … they found my beautiful Stephen. And that's the day I died. And that's the date they put on his gravestone.

A friend told me about Roland. She said he was coming to her place in Norwell, Massachusetts. She said to please come. She hoped I might receive a message from Stephen or at the very least some explanation of what transpired that fateful day.

"Yes, I will come," I told her. I wanted to know what happened to my Stephen. I knew he had low blood sugar, but what happened? Why couldn't he make it home?

So I made plans to see this man who shared spiritual communications and hear what he might have to say. My first impression of him made me smile. I had months and months of never smiling and for some reason this man made me smile. I think I figured he was enlightened in some way and maybe he could help me. I could feel Stephen with me and I even had many experiences that made me know he was with me, but for some reason I was waiting for something else, something that Stephen wanted me to hear.

That evening Roland came directly to me and said, "Your husband did not drown—he died before he hit the water." Roland touched his fingertip and said, "He doesn't have to do this anymore," as he mimicked someone testing his blood sugar. "He bottomed out—his blood sugar bottomed out."

The tears rolled down my face and I wanted to know more.

Roland handed me my first Purple Paper, dated March 1, 2013. It said, "I am safe in heaven. I know no one knows what happened, but I am in heaven." Oh my God, this is what I needed to hear. I pressed that Purple Paper to my heart. It was magical to me. Roland had drawn the pond area and with it the trees and the water and the bright light going into the water. I just couldn't let go of this Purple Paper. And although Roland always says, "You don't need me to get a message from your loved ones," I do know that to be true. But it was those Purple Papers that drew me back and kept drawing me back. They are, for me, letters from heaven.

My second Purple Paper, dated March 9, 2013, told me more of the story: "The water came over me. I didn't have time to get out. I saw the light, then passed away. I really found heaven." This picture was of the water, a figure in the water, and three hearts around him. The light was coming down on him again. It gave me peace. It was another piece of the puzzle.

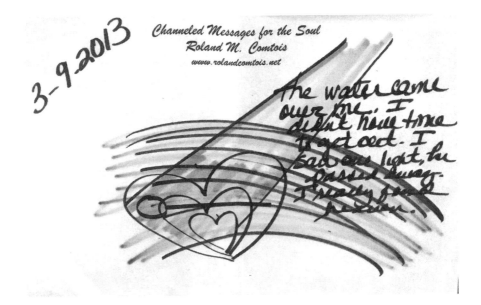

"Please God, have him give me more," I begged, "so I can know what happened." I would never rest without knowing.

My third visit was a heavy one for me. I kept worrying if my Stephen had suffered. Someone must have known that was on my mind because the Purple Paper dated July 22, 2013, that Roland handed me that night said, "You need to know that I was not in the car, but I did not feel pain." The picture was of my husband's car at the water with three stars in the sky. He did not feel pain. Thank you.

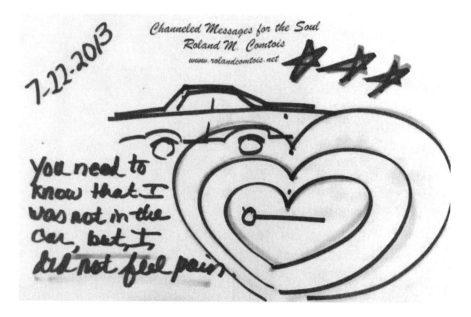

I got a lot of signs from Stephen from day one. He seemed frantic to let me know he was OK. That's what I felt anyway in my heart. And yet I kept asking, are these cardinal birds really from you, Steve?

Soon it was time to go again and see if there would be a Purple Paper for me. This one was dated August 12, 2013, and there was a picture of a bird on it. The writing on it said, "So, my wife will ask you, 'Did my husband really send me the bird in the yard?' Tell her 'YES.'"

Channeled Messages for the Soul
Roland M. Comtois
www.rolandcomtois.net

8-12-2013

So, my wife will ask you, "Did my husband really send me the bird in the yard?" Tell her "YES."

Well, you cannot get clearer than that... Oh yes, you can... Oh yes, you can...

It was my birthday, June 21, 2014. My son Jeff asked what I wanted for my birthday. I knew he was suffering as I was. I said, "Jeff, I would like you to come to see Roland with me for my birthday." It didn't take much convincing, but I knew he was a little skeptical at first. While we were driving, we agreed that Jeff would ask his dad to mention my birthday. No one else was there.

During the presentation, Roland said, "Is it someone's birthday?" Jeff looked at me—and then Roland said, "Does your name begin with C? I am hearing C." Yes, it does begin with C, but more than that—my husband called me "Ce." Just "Ce" and it was my birthday. Jeff damn near fell off his chair. The paper had June 21, 2014, on it. Around the date was a C in quotation marks. The picture was the pond with the water, the trees, and a figure in the water, like the others with the three hearts. It said, "I tried so hard to stay strong for you. I tried so hard to keep myself together. I found the angels because of you." This was the most special paper I was to receive.

But remember, Stephen was missing for a week. I was in such anguish and my soul has never recovered. I saw Roland again and received another life-changing message. The Purple Paper was very specific for what I was thinking of... they always are. Dated July 22, 2014, the paper said, "1-2-3-4 days, 5-6-7 days. I passed away without struggling. The water was cold. You can never blame yourself." Slowly, the puzzle was coming together, and my questions were being answered.

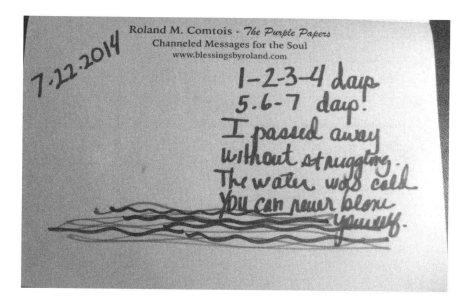

The last paper I received, dated February 23, 2015, had a picture of water—just rippled water—and this time there was no figure in the water. It was gone. The writing said, "Someone helped me from the water. It was like a light. I got lost a little bit, then I felt a light or something. I didn't know about the 'light,' but I really felt it."

There is no denying that love never dies. There is no denying that our loved ones truly are alive on the other side, and they talk to us and see us. If we open ourselves up, we can experience that love and know they are with us always. For me, the Purple Papers were a key. They helped me open the door to the other side. I have always had experiences since I was a child—but they were buried somewhere in my heart. When Stephen died, it was as if someone told Roland to give me the keys. And every Purple Paper he gave me brought me closer to peace.

Chapter 9

OUR SEPARATE WAYS
BY ROSEANN BABELLI

Joe was determined to fulfill his personal dream of becoming more than a police detective. He certainly was on his way and could've earned a greater status, but sadly by his own hands he died at a young age.

Joe and I dated for about a year. There was no explanation at the time for why our relationship ended other than the fact that he "wasn't happy." It was like a switch was turned off and it was over. I didn't understand his unhappiness at the time. He was a quiet man but had a sense of humor. I did not know he suffered from depression until after the revelation of his death.

After we broke up, we both went on to marry other people rather quickly. I ran into him only once after we went our separate ways. He looked so sad. I felt he had a lot to say to me, but it remained unsaid. I never saw him again.

I remember being stunned by the news that Joe had taken his own life. He was buried nearby, and I felt such a yearning to search for his grave. It was an unusually warm day. It had rained the night before, so the ground was all muddy. I came to a certain spot and was stopped by some unseen force.

When I started to doubt myself, I visualized two gold letters with Joe's initials in my hand. I was breathless, got on my knees and began to scrape the mud off the plaque. Joe guided me. I was in the right place all along.

A year later, I was in my laundry room and Joe appeared to me. It was only for about ten seconds. He was wearing a navy-blue suit and white shirt, and his tie was undone. I focused on the tie. A year later, I had a psychic reading. The medium described everything Joe was wearing, and Joe said, "I never liked that tie. I wanted to be buried in my uniform." That is when I knew that Joe had something to say that was bigger than I could have possibly imagined. What he could not tell me in life, he said in death.

Nearly twenty years later, I attended a Purple Paper event. Roland spoke of a police officer. Just like the feeling I had at the cemetery, I knew Joe had a message for me. Joe came through again.

The message said, "Joe didn't want to talk about how he was feeling. I never wanted you to be overwhelmed with what I had to go through. Maybe I should've taken better care of myself throughout the years. 1975 was a tough time. Today I am peaceful. (Repeat that to them.)"

7. 11. 2017 Roland M. Comtois - *The Purple Papers*
www.RolandComtois.net

Joe didn't want to talk about how he was feeling. I never wanted you to be overwhelmed with what I had to go through. Maybe I shouldn't taken better care of myself through out the years. 1975 was a tough time. Today I am peaceful. (Repeat that to them.)

Now I understand what Joe couldn't tell me. The message was surprising, comforting and shocking all at once … magnified by one million. It was something I needed to hear. It affirmed my beliefs that our loved ones are still here with us, always embracing us with love that never dies.

Chapter 10

A MYSTERIOUS FLIGHT

BY RUTH MCINTOSH

My husband, Jack, was an intelligent, quiet person who took life seriously not only in his work but in our family as well. He kept his emotions to himself and didn't talk much in social settings, so to others he may have been seen as a loner. But I always felt a deep strength in him and knew that whatever the eventuality, he would take care of things.

The times he would really enjoy himself and let his heart shine through were when he played with our children, participated in sports, or flew our plane. At the time of his death he was an engineer and a highly qualified pilot, coming in second in the world in acrobatics, and also served as safety consultant for Beechcraft Aircraft. In addition, he was in the process of establishing a flight cargo transport service. His hopes for the future soared as he followed through on his plans with the same dedication and commitment he showed in everything he did.

But one day it all came crashing down as I answered a call from the US Coast Guard. They told me Jack had called in a Mayday from the company plane while flying between Florida and the Bahamas. He gave his bearings and turned off all radio equipment because there was a fire in the cockpit, as was the standard procedure. Search and rescue went out that day and the next day found only parts of a flap of the plane that had gone down. Jack's body was never recovered.

I have always believed in life after death, and so over these years, I had gone to other mediums in hopes of receiving a message from my husband. I never received a message through them, but that did not stop me from talking to Jack every now and then to ask for his help with our two, now grown, daughters' problems. Strange, but at times I have felt closer to him after his death than while we were married.

When I had the opportunity to attend a presentation given by Roland, I went and again hoped that I might receive a message. I sensed an excitement of some sort in the room, and I just couldn't help smiling when Roland finally appeared. His approach was different from what I had experienced before because he did it in such an upbeat, loving, and caring way. At the first break, I won a copy of his book, and while accepting it at the front desk, I noticed the Purple Papers. I was invited to look through them. The second Purple Paper was a picture of a plane moving downward from the sky with yellow flames around the plane. The date of this presentation was written on the top of the page. I said, "This might apply to me," and suddenly Roland came up to me and said, "I have been waiting for you. May I share this with the group?" Interestingly, I was supposed to go to a different one of Roland's presentations, but due to a car accident, I was able to change it to this date.

Roland told me that Jack had been trying to communicate with me for a long time. He told me he has been there for our girls. He confirmed that the accident had nothing to do with his skills and that he was an accomplished pilot, as I had already known. He further said not to worry about the body. This last one really startled me because over the years, I had not told anyone, but it had bothered me that, somehow, he just might still be alive. Although I would intellectualize the accident and know this could not be the case, there were two occasions when I thought I had seen him while I was working out of state. Because of this, I had realized I had not really accepted his death on some level. But now tears came to my eyes upon hearing this as I now finally and totally accepted his death. Roland may have said more but I was too lost in this information, which meant so much to me. I was able to come to terms with his death, a gift of peace of mind that is truly priceless.

Chapter 11

LOVE REMAINS

BY JANINE A. PASSARETTI

When I lost my beloved husband, Michael, two years ago very suddenly and tragically, I went to see Roland a few months afterward. Michael had been only forty-six years old and was a happy and healthy man who loved his family more than anything. We were married for twenty years. We had three beautiful daughters together. Our worlds were turned upside down the day he took his own life without warning or any indication why. We know it was a mental breakdown, and for us it came out of nowhere. It was like being hit by an Acela train in the middle of a silent, snow-filled forest.

I received a Purple Paper from Roland not only on one occasion but multiple times. Michael wanted to make sure Roland delivered his messages to my girls and me. Michael was sorry, and he couldn't get his "head right." Everything that was conveyed in the Purple Paper messages could only have come through Michael.

The papers, five different ones, and the messages that were delivered would prove to bring me peace in the fact that I know that Michael is not gone. He is with us in some way. Love does not die. Love remains...love is eternal, as Roland says. I believe this to be true.

The first time I received a Purple Paper from Roland was right after Michael's death. I was in search of something, anything that could bring me peace (if that was even possible). When I saw Roland, Michael came through first during a small group event. Roland mentioned someone that passed through a suicide. He said, "Michael Anthony." I knew it was him. The paper mentioned that he was "sorry about the gun." Roland went on to say that Michael said his "head wasn't right" and he "didn't hurt anymore." Michael committed suicide by a gunshot wound. He died days shy of our twentieth wedding anniversary.

4-11-2016

Roland M. Comtois - *The Purple Papers*
Channeled Messages for the Soul
www.blessingsbyroland.com

I'm sorry about the gun.
I'm sorry about the gun.
I'm sorry about the gun.

"Michael is so sorry that he did what he did. I wanted to get it cleared up, but I couldn't. I'm so happy now that my 'head' doesn't hurt. You were so good to me," read a Purple Paper from December 1, 2015. Another repeated his earlier message: "I'm sorry about the gun. I'm sorry about the gun. I'm sorry about the gun."

5-10-2016

Roland M. Comtois - *The Purple Papers*
Channeled Messages for the Soul
www.blessingsbyroland.com

Michael Anthony
There was nothing you
could do. I want you to
know that before anything else.
I know how hard you always tried.
When I send a sign you feel it
just. Don't you always feel me.
I love you

The next paper was from May 10, 2016: "Michael Anthony. There was nothing you could do. I want you to know that before anything else. I know how hard you always tried. When I send a sign, you feel it first. You always feel me. I love you."

The other paper actually showed a picture of our bedroom and where I was praying with him that last night and burning candles because he had not been himself for a little over a week. The next day he would be gone forever. Roland said things that only I would know. He even took on Michael's persona. He grabbed my shoulders and repeatedly said, "I love you so much." That was very much him. He also said he is "OK" and he made it to heaven. He even said, "I found Grandma."

My grandmother passed just five days prior to Michael's death. It was as if Michael were answering all the questions I would repeatedly ask him at night while I was alone. I also received other papers via my family who were at an event of Roland's when I had gone away to England to visit my friends for what would have been our twentieth wedding anniversary and I was hurting so much. The pain I was in was excruciating. I didn't want to be anywhere familiar without him.

When I returned from England, I had a need to attend another event. Roland delivered another Purple Paper that night. It said, "Michael. Yes, I made it home. Yes, I made it to heaven. Yes, I found peace. Yes, I'm happy. I hope that answers all of your questions … Of course, I'll watch out for you." It also had a note on the top right corner that said, "Keep telling her. She really needs to hear it over and over again." Though it has been a very long road, the messages that I have received via Roland have been nothing less than a miracle to me. They have given me back my faith when I was losing it, as well as all hope.

5-10-2016

Roland M. Comtois - *The Purple Papers*
Channeled Messages for the Soul
www.blessingsbyroland.com

(KEEP TELLING HER.
She really need to
hear it over and
over again.)

Michael

YES I made it home.
YES I made it to heaven.
YES I found peace.
YES I'm happy.
I hope that answers all of
your questions... Of course, I'll
watch out for you

I have always been a woman of faith, but the pain and despair I felt was like nothing I could even fathom. Nor did I ever believe I would have faith in anything again. The message helped me realize that love doesn't die and our loved ones don't just go away. They are with us always.

Chapter 12

DNR

BY JUNE

The day I received my Purple Paper, I also was blessed with much needed, life-changing peace. I have been carrying around an inescapable heaviness in my heart for years about my cousin Margret's passing, and the message she sent lifted it from me that day. Ten years older than me, Margret was my best friend and took me under her wing when my mother passed away in 1987. I was only twenty-seven at the time and my mother was just fifty-six. My world had shattered with her passing.

Instinctively intuitive and compassionate, Margret knew how broken I was after my mother's death and took it upon herself to help me through this difficult time with spiritual teachings, healing, and a lot of laughs. She also introduced me to the world of Reiki. Combining the Japanese words *rei*, meaning spiritual wisdom, and *ki*, life force energy, *Reiki* is a technique that uses spiritually guided life force energy for stress reduction and relaxation and also promotes emotional and physical healing. It is administered by laying on hands and is based on the idea that an unseen life force energy (the ki) flows through us and is what causes us to be alive. If our life force energy is low, then we are more likely to get sick or feel stress, and if it is high, we are more capable of being happy and healthy. Reiki and my cousin were godsends for me as I began to heal from the pain of my mother's death.

Years later, the tables turned and my cousin needed my help when she was diagnosed with breast cancer. In keeping with her beliefs, she fought it through natural and holistic ways. I remember celebrating her being five years cancer free. We thought we had conquered it forever!

No matter how hard we wish and pray, some things are out of our control. Several years later, her cancer returned in her lungs. Wanting to make things easier for everyone in the event of the inevitable and no longer being able to speak for herself, she wrote her living will. She let us know that she had signed a Do Not Resuscitate (DNR) order and made us all understand her intentions. A DNR is a legal order written to withhold cardiopulmonary resuscitation (CPR) or life support in respect of the wishes of a patient in case their heart were to stop or they were to stop breathing. Margret did not want to be kept alive should her heart or breathing stop. I didn't want to think about that, but I told her I would support her wishes.

When that terrible day came, her family fought the hospital and put my cousin on life support. None of us were ready to let her go, but it was not our decision to make. When I went to the hospital, it broke my heart to see her wishes not being met. I sat with her parents, my aunt and uncle, and gently reminded them of her wishes. It was such an emotional time. After some painful soul searching and shared tears, they agreed to disconnect her from life support. Twenty minutes later she was pronounced dead. I struggled with my part in that day and carried the burden and heartbreak for years. When I received a message from her on Roland's Purple Paper, I knew my cousin was at a place of peace and I didn't have to shoulder that burden any longer.

I lost my cousin thirteen years after I lost my mother, losing my footing in life too. I found it again on June 5, 2010, when Roland gave me a message, heaven sent. It read, "It's OK that you pulled the plug. I told you a long time ago—it would be OK."

Channeled Messages for the Soul
Roland M. Comtois
401-647-4446
www.blessingsbyroland.com

6/5/2010

It's OK that you pulled the plug. I told you a long time ago — it would be OK

Chapter 13

I'VE GOT MY BOY

BY MARYALICE

It had been nine years since I received messages from my loved ones from Roland. My brother Ritchie died tragically at the age of two and a half after being struck by a dump truck in front of our home. I was only four years old at the time, and we both had been playing across the street. My mom came to get Ritchie for his afternoon nap but said I could stay there and play. Ritchie started to cry because he wanted to stay with me. The next thing I heard was screeching brakes and my mother's screams. When they had gotten to the front door, Ritchie pulled out of her hand and went running across the street right into the path of an oncoming truck. The driver was unable to stop, and Ritchie was killed instantly. This happened on March 31, 1959. Mom and I both blamed ourselves for his death.

I told myself over the years that if I had come home with him, he never would have been killed. My grandmother reassured me that Ritchie was in heaven with Grandpa, but I still carried the guilt and heartache into my adult life. Forty years later, I was going through breast cancer treatments and Mom came to spend two weeks with my family and me as I was finishing my treatments.

On March 31, a few days before her departure from my home, I found her sitting sadly on my couch. I assured her that I was fine and would survive the cancer. She said she knew I would be fine, but she had been thinking of Ritchie. It was forty years to the day since he was killed. Her heart was still aching terribly for him. We cried together, sharing our loss. A few days later, she left to go home with Dad. Dad stayed home, his fear of flying keeping him from visiting with us. Tragically, she had a heart attack halfway across the Pacific and died before landing in Los Angeles. Again, my heart was broken in two. Mom was my best friend, who taught us all unconditional love.

I went to see Roland in June 2008, hoping to connect with my mother, Dad (who had since passed), and Ritchie. Roland shared with me that they were there, along with my grandparents and multiple angels, and that they were all watching over me. I had no doubt he was speaking with Mom because he described her personality perfectly, saying she was soft spoken and had waited patiently for her turn to come forward. That was my mother. She thanked me, saying how proud she was of how I helped my siblings and dad get through her passing and that I was the strength and the rock. Her special love came through, and I was reminded by the angels that we were all blessed by the unconditional love she taught us to share. Roland then told me he had a Purple Paper from her to me in his never-ending stack of papers at the front of the room. How he would find it in all those binders was beyond my comprehension. He searched through them during the break, and I cried when he showed me what Mom had told him on June 25, a few days before our gathering.

It was a drawing of an angel's wings with a large red heart in the center, surrounded by the words, "The angels healed my heavy heart. I've got my boy with me." I cried, but at the same time, all the forty-eight years of pain were lifted from my heart. This paper is my most cherished gift. The experience opened the door and cleared the pathway for me to progress on my spiritual journey. I know my mom is always at my side. She sends me cardinals (her favorite bird) and I feel her hugs and hear her gentle words as I continue on my earthly journey knowing we will be together in spirit someday.

Channeled Messages for the Soul
Roland M. Comtois
401-647-4446
www.blessingsbyroland.com

6/25/08

The angels healed my heavy heart. I've got my boy with me

Chapter 14

WITH THE ANGELS

BY SHERRYL FIELDS

A number of years ago, my good friend Diane invited me to attend an event featuring Roland at a small artsy space in Woonsocket, Rhode Island. After the show, when most everyone had left, Diane and I sat down at a table and had a glass of wine. While we were sitting there, Roland came over and joined us. Diane introduced me to Roland and they chatted a bit. Suddenly, Roland looked at me and said, "I have a Purple Paper for you."

Then he jumped up and headed toward the back of the building. Diane looked at me with wide eyes. Wow! This was exciting and totally unexpected. I wasn't really sure what this was going to mean but I could feel a stirring of emotions inside, like there was some impending information that was going to be revealed. It felt like something I was dying to hear, but at the same time I dreaded it because I knew the overwhelming emotions that would come with it.

Many thoughts flashed through my mind as I waited for Roland to return with the paper. He sat down and laid the drawing in front of me. Written upon the page was the date October 3, 2010, and it said, "Your baby is with the angels." He proceeded to tell me that the daughter we had lost in 1993 when I was six months into my first pregnancy was now safe and living and growing with the angels in heaven. He said that she was watching over us and our three boys. She was working so hard behind the scenes to guide us and heal us from our earthly pain.

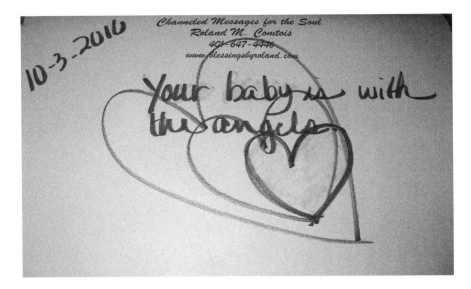

I asked Roland why she didn't stay with us. He said that she had her own work to do and that she was doing it from the other side but that she is always around us and is sending us her love and guidance. He explained that we all come with our own mission to accomplish and that our presence or absence affects other people's work as well. He said that she had to go through the process of coming into this life and leaving it for her own growth and development as a soul.

This loss was so very difficult in many ways. I had waited my entire life to have this first baby and expected to get to keep her. It was my first pregnancy, and I was deathly sick the entire time (as I was with all of them). She was a girl. I went on to have three boys. I have always wondered how our lives would have been different if she, Shelby, had stayed. Having Roland explain his understanding of her life brought some relief and helped me understand that sometimes there is a bigger plan that we are only just a part of.

I will always miss her and long for her, but I do believe that someday all the answers will be revealed to us and we will understand. It was a blessing to get that Purple Paper and feel connected to my baby even for just those few moments.

Chapter 15

I LOVE MY BEACH
BY BILL GROSS

Many years ago during the turbulent Vietnam era of the 1960s, the loss of a president, and the beginning of a time of protest, there was a haven for those lucky enough to live in Rye, New York, in a neighborhood called Oakland Park. At the time it was the home of a beautiful beach, a duck pond, rolling green gentle hills and Oakland Pool. Most of today's residents and visitors would deny there was a pool, but those who lived in Rye and grew up in the fifties and sixties would quickly correct them. It was there, and it graced the park with its beauty and relief from the long, hot summers of those days.

My future wife, Denise, was then a little girl, and she played in the park, her fantasyland, a wondrous place to explore and a safe refuge from the challenges of growing up. She lived a half a block from the beach and spent pretty much every summer day playing in the water, climbing out on the jetty, and learning to swim at Oakland Pool.

As the years went by, this little girl grew to be a tall, beautiful young woman and a superb swimmer. It was a time when women were mostly relegated to support roles; rarely would one think of a woman as a potential lifesaver, unless of course she worked in nursing. But this woman was a pioneer of sorts and, I'm proud to say, was the first female lifeguard at Oakland Pool.

For endless summer days, she sat atop the guard chair, complete with zinc oxide protecting her nose and lips, watching every movement in the pool. It was, she said, a place of great pride coupled with a sense of accomplishment. One day, she and her colleagues saved a young woman with special needs who panicked and fought them as they gently wrestled her back to safety. In all her humility and humanity, she wore a radiant smile and felt a profound satisfaction that she had helped to save a life.

Denise would often bring me and our children to her special park and her special beach, telling us about the ducks and her wonderful fantasyland. And then she walked us down Dearborn Avenue, past what was once a deli known as Warrens, down to the end where the pool once was. It's hard to accept change, but she told us many times that despite the absence of the pool, the heart and beauty of Oakland Park remained.

I need to add that she became my wife and for thirty-two years filled my heart and those of our children with her lifesaving nature. Denise LaMedica Gross, a beautiful woman of inestimable warmth and love, passed from this world in April 2008.

But she didn't leave us.

I know that for many reasons, the most tangible of which came from Roland during a presentation I attended a few years after Denise had passed when he handed me a Purple Paper he said was for me. The words written on it said it all: "Thank you for bringing me to the beach."

All I could do was nod through my tears. I knew the message was from Denise and I understood its importance to her, to me, to our children. It captured a lifetime of love and lessons learned, and it gave me the courage and the confidence to carry on as she wished I would.

Denise passed as she had lived, in the gentle loving embrace of those she loved unconditionally and those who love her endlessly still. My wife was my best half, the amazing mother of our two beautiful children, a healer in every sense of the word, and a devoted friend to those who had the honor and privilege to share her life. She was fifty-seven years young.

You don't realize what you have when you have it. That's probably one of the first thoughts I had after she had gone. The second was that I didn't think I could ever get over the loss of someone I loved with every fiber of my being.

Denise blessed us every minute in many ways and still does. I feel it all the time.

I met Denise when I was twenty-five, fresh off a bad marriage that sent me screaming from relationships. I was a hippie from the sixties and I was a mess. She was a stewardess for American Airlines, sophisticated, worldly, beautiful inside and out, a complex, spiritual woman who knocked me over in every shape and form. I came to her as a boy and left as a man.

I never knew what it was like to be in love before Denise. But as we began our life together, we embarked on what turned out to be one of *the* great love affairs.

We married in 1976 and began a journey that would take us from Brooklyn to the Midwest and eventually to Connecticut as we followed my tumultuous career in the film and advertising businesses. Everything we did during the earlier years of our marriage centered on me. No matter how chaotic or disconcerting our situation was or how many times I uprooted the family while I chased my dreams, Denise brought it all together for us.

And she did it for years and years without even the hint of a complaint until one day she turned and looked at me and very calmly said, "You need to grow up, Bill, do your job, and become an equal partner is this marriage."

Here I was out running after acting jobs, while she stayed home day into night with two children, and I hadn't given a thought to her needs, to what she might want to do for her life.

She informed me that she had enrolled in an English course that met every Tuesday night, and she would need me to be home to take care of the kids while she was out. As it turned out, it not only made our relationship stronger, it became healthier in every respect. The more she followed her dreams, the more she blossomed, and I was more amazed by her than ever.

She began to study Reiki, a healing touch practice that meshed with every part of her. Reiki is a Japanese technique for stress reduction and relaxation that also promotes healing. A relatively simple technique to learn, the ability to use Reiki is not taught in the usual sense but is transferred to the student during a Reiki class. This ability is passed on during an "attunement" given by a Reiki Master and allows the student to tap into an unlimited supply of life force energy to improve one's health and enhance the quality of life.

Denise's Reiki Master was Roland Comtois, and his teaching gifts extended far beyond the classroom. After attending one of his presentations for the first time, Denise came home completely enthralled. It was like a switch was turned on.

She talked to me about visualization and meditation and Roland, suggesting that a combination of the three could help me realize my dreams of becoming an actor. She even gave me a gift of a session with Roland so I could experience for myself his visions and counsel.

I was not sure I believed in any of this, but to please Denise I went to see him. As soon as I walked into the room, he instantly started to speak of the people he saw standing with me. "There's a lovely lady here who wants to hug you. She's light and loving and loves you," he said.

I knew at once he was talking about my mom. I was born in 1949 to an unwed mother, a beautiful vivacious woman who loved me unconditionally and defied convention to raise me on her own, then with the man who would become my beloved stepfather. I never knew my birth father in life, but I was about to meet him through Roland.

"There's a man in the room who wants me to tell you how sorry he is. 'I just couldn't do it,' he says. His name is Ed."

Ed was my birth father's name. He was an Irishman and that was basically all I had known about him. But that one session with Roland helped me deal with and heal unresolved issues about him that I had carried with me all my life.

After my experience with Roland, I began to better understand what was driving Denise's evolution to fully embrace spirituality. At the same time, I fearfully wondered if her new beliefs and her Reiki training would take her away from me. In fact, it did the opposite. Reiki became a lifeline for our family and for many others whose lives Denise touched.

She took advanced Reiki training with Roland in Rhode Island, returning home with a gift that gave life back, instead of taking it away. As a Reiki practitioner, she used her healing touch expertise on patients in the cancer center of our local hospital, instinctively knowing how Reiki therapy could help ease their pain, and maybe intuitively feeling an unbidden kinship with their illness.

It seemed almost out of nowhere when the tables turned on her and she became the patient. She was diagnosed with breast cancer not once but twice.

She underwent chemo and all the other unkind treatments that ravaged her body. And she beat it…for a time.

She began to feel sick again but refused to give in to the pain. She wanted to enjoy all the positive opportunities that life presented to her. I remember she wanted to go on a weeklong meditation retreat about that same time in spite of her declining health. Her doctor was worried and wanted to check her numbers before she left. After meeting with him at his office, Denise became uncharacteristically quiet and sad. She did not go on the trip that she was very much looking forward to.

Two days later we learned that she had an inoperable mass in her pancreas. There was no hope of recovery.

"I will not make any concessions to this illness," she told me emphatically after hearing the news, adding that "we can't let it rule our lives. We, you and I together, will dance at our daughter's wedding. We will carry on."

Our daughter was getting married a few months after Denise's diagnosis shattered our lives. Denise was more than determined not to let her cancer stand in the way. We sought out a second opinion from the finest doctors only to be told that they could not do anything more for Denise. Denise elected to fight her illness spiritually. She didn't want to, but she took pain medicine to help her get through the days until our daughter's wedding. Everything about that magical day was truly heaven made, and Denise was as radiant as our daughter was. When the band played and the dancing began, she danced with the kind of happiness that transcends time and place, her face aglow with pure love and joy. She didn't want the moment ever to end and neither did I.

She passed quietly some months later in the spring of the following year as my heart screamed in agony. Roland visited us the day after Denise died, feeling compelled to comfort and assure us that Denise would always be with us, that the bonds of love were eternal. He asked to speak with me privately and inexplicably proceeded to repeat intimate conversations I had with Denise in the days before she passed. There was no way he could have made up the words he shared with me. I knew Denise must have shared them with Roland from the other side, to send me the message that she would always be with me. It knocked me over.

In the weeks and months that followed, our family was a chaotic mess. I tried to rationalize to the kids, to myself, the reason that Mom was not with us, telling them she needed to be where she was. None of us accepted or understood that, but there was nothing else we could do to change it. As Denise had wanted, I had her remains cremated. The kids and I talked about where we would spread her ashes, where she would be the happiest. We agreed that we would bring her back to the beach where she grew up, to a place where Mom took us all and showed us where she wanted to build her dream house when she was a young girl.

We hugged, we cried, and we prayed as the three of us scattered her ashes to the wind, sand, and sea some days later. I wrote a piece about her love for this beach, a tribute to a young girl full of hope, love, and eternal sunshine, making her an indelible part of the seascape that meant so much to her in life and now in death. I read it to her there that day.

The phone rang just as we returned home. It was Roland. "She's all around," he said. "She said you went to the right place."

While Roland checked in from time to time after that day, I didn't see him again until I had the opportunity to attend a presentation he was doing in a historic mansion in Norwalk for a TV show. He didn't know I was coming.

I sat in the audience of forty with my ever-present heavy heart, listening to the people around me get messages from loved ones they had lost, feeling their grief and their emotions as Roland shared stories long past, many of which were written on the Purple Papers he carries with him wherever he goes.

Then he stopped in front of me. "I have a Purple Paper for you." He held it up. On it was a drawing of a seashore and the words I will never forget: "I love my beach. I love the morning sun. I love standing near the trees at home."

It gives me comfort to know that we brought her happiness as she did to those who knew and loved her. And I do believe that she is always around us. I sense her presence when I need her the most. I feel her gently guiding me to move forward, take a chance on life again, to love again. I see her every day, in my kids and in my grandchildren. We had a nickname for her: we

called her "Vinnie." Now my grandson shares that name with her. She loved and lived with all her heart, an angel whose time here was just part of a longer journey. She once told me that during one of her Reiki sessions at the hospital, she felt someone come into the room while she was working on her patient. She was pretty sure it was Jesus. I didn't understand that at the time, but now, considering how she devoted her life to saving others, it makes sense to me. I think Denise was preparing us for her inevitable departure and making us stronger while she was here. She still is.

Chapter 16

HEAVEN IS REAL

BY DEBBIE COLES

I received my Purple Paper in August 2012 at a group event with Roland in Rhode Island, which was amazing by itself because I wasn't even supposed to be in town that week. But somehow, I found myself right there, where I needed to be—the recipient of a Purple Paper. The message Roland had received was from my man Jimmy, who had crossed over fourteen years earlier in 1998.

While there weren't any shocking revelations on the message, what was written there on my Purple Paper confirmed what I had experienced after his passing. Jimmy had not believed in the afterlife during his time on earth, so when he mentioned how he believed in heaven now, I was both amused and delighted, especially since it confirmed that he was safe—and there.

He also said that he visited me seventeen nights after he passed.

I have always remembered that visit, vividly and distinctly, but the people I shared it with told me that I had been dreaming. When Jimmy appeared to me, I was drowning in guilt and confusion about what had taken place just before his death. Hopeless that I couldn't save him. I was lying in bed with my mind spinning. I couldn't envision him any other way but how I found him. Then suddenly I could feel and smell him in such a comforting angelic way that I had never felt. It was like I was floating with him. I could fully feel everything about him without the physical touch. Once that happened, all my thoughts turned to knowing he was OK and at peace. He began to leave and the mist that surrounded him slowly dissipated. I felt he didn't want to scare me but wanted to give me comfort to move on. Roland says the difference between a dream and a visit is the clarity with which you can remember every single detail, all the colors, expressions, movements, and more, as if it had taken place a minute ago right in front of your own eyes. I knew without a doubt in my heart that it was real and Jimmy confirmed it in his message to me.

Roland also drew a picture of me in my bed sleeping. The lamp on the nightstand next to my bed started flickering soon after he passed and still does today. Roland picked up on that and said that's Jimmy checking in and letting me know he is always watching over me. I have always felt that, but Roland confirmed it for me.

Even now, twenty years later, Jimmy still makes an appearance and sends me signs to remind me he'll always be watching over me. For that, I'm very grateful.

Chapter 17

TREASURED FRIEND
BY SWEETGRASS

I met Roland through my treasured teacher, Helen, who believed in sharing joy and healing energy with divine purpose. It came as no surprise that she encouraged me to attend one of Roland's presentations. It was Halloween. My daughter and I came dressed in costumes. I wasn't exactly sure what would transpire that night, but I was ready to receive any gifts that would come my way. That's when I received my first Purple Paper, transcribed weeks in advance and well before I had any knowledge or intention of attending.

The message was simple in its brevity, but the meaning it held was personally and profoundly gratifying. It said, "My granddaughter has my family recipes." A drawing on the Purple Paper was of a simple brown box with black lettering, the exact depiction of the recipe box I received from my grandmother, the box I cherish with all my heart. She passed in 1981. She was my maternal grandmother and the person with whom I felt most loved. I loyally use her recipes, some in her own shaky handwriting, and am so grateful for her gift. I was extremely close to my grandmother. The box was gifted to me during our lifetime together. Her message delivered, my greatest treasure, on the Purple Paper was another timeless reminder of our enduring love.

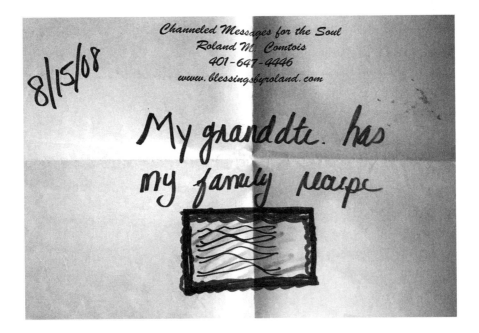

A sudden loss motivated me to attend another Purple Paper event. My father tragically died after choking at a celebratory dinner of champagne and foie gras. He was placed on a respirator, against his wishes, never to regain consciousness and dying soon thereafter.

Once again, my treasured teacher encouraged me to attend an event. It was a gray, rainy evening, but the potential of a blessing encouraged me to venture out. Finally, I made my way into the room, filled with people praying for their own blessing. Roland picked me out of the crowd of fifty. What happened next was chilling and telling. The Purple Paper, again depicted with accuracy, was my father's plight in his last days. A drawing of a man hooked up to wires with the words "He fought—He did not want it." That I knew referred to the life support actions that were issued. "Harvey is peaceful!" read the next message I received that night. I was glad to know that my father reached out to me and assured me that he was at peace. I needed that.

The woman who guided me on my journey from grief and loss to peace and acceptance was waging her own life-threatening battle. I, along with others who loved Helen, were at her side when she passed, supporting and lov-

ing one another with all the strength and compassion we could muster when our hearts were breaking. My next Purple Paper held a message from Helen. She told me that she would send me a feather so I would know that she was thinking of me.

A year and half went by before I found my feather. I was walking to a bus stop on my way to the hospital for yet another back surgery. My pain had not let up and I desperately hoped there would be relief this time. There at my feet was an amazing brown feather. I knew it was from Helen. She would be with me during the procedure. I thanked her silently and made my way into the hospital. I am now virtually pain free, the first time in about ten years, and I believe Helen had a hand in my healing.

I had the opportunity to see Roland once again and was more than delighted to receive another Purple Paper. It was from Helen. Through Roland, she wrote:

"My dear sister, you were so smart about what I needed and how to help. I really didn't have pain. You were a treasured friend."

My Purple Papers were my constant solace during decades of suffering from undiagnosed PTSD. They and Helen remain invaluable treasures.

Chapter 18

MY DAD'S RED JEEP

BY MEREDITH MCKELL GRAFF

I met Roland in early June 2014, when he was a speaker at the Afterlife Awareness Conference held that year in Portland, Oregon. Roland offered a small group session for seventeen during the open period on one afternoon. I felt compelled to register for this group. I wanted to get any information I could about my father, who died in 2009 following a horrific automobile accident. It wasn't the kind of usual car accident involving two or more vehicles. Instead, my dad, a retired botany professor, had volunteered to fix all the broken sprinklers in his condominium neighborhood.

My dad Cyrus McKell was standing on the sidewalk on the corner of his street in Utah, fixing one of the broken sprinklers on the little hill at the neighborhood entrance, in front of the sign *Mt. Olympus Condos* when he was hit from behind by his elderly neighbor, who had lost control of his car and had driven off the road onto the sidewalk. Because of the car's high rate of speed, my dad went into the windshield, up over the top of the car, sliding off to be dragged by the back wheels across the street, where the car drove over him as it continued down the opposite sidewalk. From the 911 transcripts, it seemed my dad may have died, but came back between the impact and shortly before the ambulance arrived. The trauma

ICU doctor told me later that he had his eyes open when he came into the ER and was able to blink to tell them he had no feeling in his extremities.

I got word of the accident in Washington and arranged to fly to Utah to be with him. I had no idea how badly hurt he was. I arrived in the evening and it wasn't until 10 p.m. that my mother and I were able to go into his room. His head was heavily bandaged, and I could see his heart monitor line leap when we walked into the room and started talking to him. He was blanketed, and we did not see his other injuries. I was able to sit with him for the next two and a half hours, until he peacefully died with me holding his left hand. I thought I could see figures at the foot of his bed. When he passed, it felt to me like I was handing him off to the figures like a baton in a relay race. I learned many months later the figures were my grandparents.

I went to a group channeling session a few weeks after I read the police report, and we did a meditation, during which I saw in my mind's eye what my dad saw when he was hit. He was bounced out of his body and found himself in a beautiful meadow. As he was wondering how he got there and admiring all the stunning colors and plants he didn't know, four figures walked out from trees bordering the meadow. As they got closer, I could see they were his brother, Lynn, who died at four years old but manifested as fourteen, his mother, his father, who died when my dad was eight years old, and his big brother, William, who had died only eighteen months earlier and lived to raise a wonderful family. After a huge hug (my dad, with all his Spanish-speaking-country travels, called them *abrazos*), he asked them why they were there, and they told him they had come to get him. They said, "If you want to go back to say goodbye, we will come with you and wait for you." And that is when he woke up in the gutter after being driven over by the old man's car. I saw my grandparents at the foot of my dad's bed before he died. They were there.

My dad and I were very close, and I hoped to receive a message from him when I went to Roland's small group. When I was really little, I used to tell my mother I was going to marry him someday. When I started my law firm in 2003, I used to joke that he was my silent partner. My dad was my biggest teacher, mentor, and role model.

In the small group session with Roland, we only had a couple of hours for him to get information for the seventeen people who anxiously awaited messages. I was sitting on Roland's left at the middle of a long conference table. Before he got to me, we ran out of time. Roland told me to go to dinner, the next event on the conference schedule, and then find him later for a private reading.

The first thing Roland did when we sat down together a few hours later was write on his purple pad in large letters, "I'M SORRY!" He said, "Your father wants you to know he is sorry for leaving."

I quickly responded, "He doesn't need to be sorry. I know it was his time. The way he died was too freaky for it to be anything but his time."

Roland continued, "He tells me he was ready to go but realized later you weren't ready to let him go."

I said, "He could have lived to age 100 and I still would not have been ready to let him go. It wouldn't have mattered."

"He waited for you," Roland said.

"I know," I replied.

I always knew in my heart my dad waited for me specifically. It was the kind of relationship we had. I would have waited for him too, had I been the one in the hospital bed.

After receiving information about my mother, who died almost three years after my dad, and a message from my best friend, whose ashes I put into the ocean in Hawaii after she died of lung cancer in 2010, Roland and I were wrapping up. He folded the Purple Papers on which he had written my messages, and as we talked, I noticed he had sketched a tree on the folded side. I said, "Oh my gosh, my dad is showing you the tree I planted for him last Sunday, which was the five-year anniversary of his passing." I had my iPad with me, and I got it out to show Roland the photos of the tree with the yellow ribbons I had tied on, plus the birdhouse decorated with some of the many feathers my dad has sent to me since he died.

When I got home that night, I showed my husband the Purple Papers and the drawing of the tree on the folded side. My husband asked, "What is that writing up in the corner?" I hadn't noticed writing when I saw Roland draw the tree. I read the words, "I am in the fields."

My dad had a great sense of humor and he loved jokes. One year for his birthday, I found a card that said, "You are a farmer—out standing in your field." Of course, he was outstanding in his field. My dad was the author of over three hundred books and articles and a world traveler as he consulted for Ford Foundation, Rockefeller Foundation, governments, and private entities. He was at Tiananmen Square in Beijing, China, six months after the student revolution in 1989 when Chinese troops fired on and killed hundreds of protesters. He made several trips to China, many to Mexico and South America, many to Israel, and many to Africa, and he even lived in Kenya for six months with my mother and little brother. We lived for nine months in Spain in 1968 while he was on a Fulbright Fellowship and University of California sabbatical leave. My dad was a PhD botanist and truly was outstanding in his field.

But that became a running joke, because my dad was a humble guy who introduced himself as "Cy" McKell, never Dr. McKell. His neighbors of twenty-six years (when he died) had no idea of his credentials or renowned status. My mother was mad when I approved an obituary in the *Salt Lake Tribune* that went from the top of the page to the bottom because, she said, he "never liked to toot his own horn."

I said, "He isn't tooting his own horn. I am tooting it, and if I can't toot it when he is dead, then when can I toot it?" I admired him so much. It is no wonder I got a master's in English—he used to have me edit his drafts when he was writing, whether it be a book or an article. He was a prolific writer.

My dad specialized in desert shrubs. He did a lot of fieldwork, gathering samples of rabbit brush, sage, and other desert plants for his research. Our family went on many camping trips, staying in a pop-up camper or a rented trailer in the hot Southern California desert, so he could do his research combined with a family weekend. I used to tease him that he was "just a farmer out standing in his field." I'll bet his fields now are prettier than the ones we camped in.

About two weeks after meeting Roland, I was on his Facebook page and I saw Purple Papers he had posted, hoping to find the recipients of the messages. One had a drawing of a red Jeep. I knew immediately it was my dad's red Jeep. My dad loved that red Jeep; it was the only red vehicle he had ever owned. I sent an email to Roland exclaiming, "That is my dad's red Jeep!" I called in to his radio show a few weeks later.

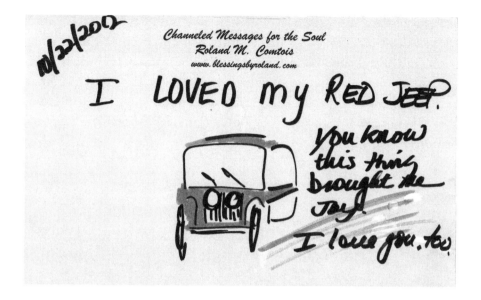

When I called in, Roland said, "You know what is really wild? I had that Purple Paper with me the day I met you in Oregon. Your dad didn't mention it."

"He wanted to have another chance to talk to me," I offered.

Roland agreed.

At his funeral, we had to shut down the viewing a half hour after the funeral was supposed to begin (the line to get in went all the way down the hall of the church corridor and around the side of the church), so we could get the funeral done and get on the road down to the Spanish Fork Cemetery, where forty retired volunteer vets (my dad's generation) were waiting to be his honor guard at his funeral. I know he loved his funeral. I felt him around the entire day. In fact, it was overcast, but it didn't start raining until the end of the lunch. It was said that my dad was "controlling the weather" because he made sure it wasn't raining at the cemetery or for most of the backyard family get-together.

I have to laugh at him because when he retired from his position as dean of science at Weber State University, he told me he was worried people would forget him. With the internet, that is not likely to happen. When I googled his name after he died, I got sixteen thousand hits. Now it is over fifty thousand. People are still quoting him in their professional papers, and his professional legacy lives on.

I am so grateful for the peace I have been given about my dad's passing. After all this time, I still miss my dad. I talk to him every day and think of him all the time. I still find feathers, but not as often as before. He still helps me find parking places in crowded parking lots. Little things every now and then let me know he is still keeping his eye on me. I am not grieving any more. These signs helped me climb out of that deep place. Now, I just look forward to seeing him again.

Chapter 19

MY MOTHER'S VOICE
BY DALE R. BELLUSCIO

One morning, I was thinking and "speaking" to my mother. She had passed only two months prior, and I was hoping she would make her presence known. I would regularly try to make a connection with her. I would try to reach out from my heart and feel her presence around me. On the night she passed, I was awoken by a shadowy figure at the foot of my bed. I was very sleepy and knew there was someone standing there but could not figure out who it was. At 7:30 a.m. the next morning, I received a phone call that my mother had passed during the night. In my heart, I knew it was she who was my overnight visitor.

I attended one of Roland's events with my sister and husband. I was nervous that within a roomful of people the likelihood that my mother would come across was probably small. I was telling myself that she had only passed a short time ago and that others in the room needed a message more than I did. My husband grabbed my hand and quietly said, "Dale, just breathe." Within minutes of the event starting, Roland turned to me and said, "Your mother is here!"

When Roland began to speak to me, the emotions came over me like a giant wave. I felt excitement, sadness, fear, and happiness all at the same time. Being a family therapist and helping countless individuals work through their grief, I intellectually knew all these emotions were my grief process rearing its head again. My mother and I had a very difficult relationship when she was here. To be accurate, we hadn't had much contact in the past twenty-five years. So for Roland to say she was present so quickly into the event was unbelievable to me. For years, I felt in my heart that my mother was angry and hated me. And here she was in this room speaking to me through Roland. To be honest, because of the emotional state I was in, I heard only about half of what Roland was saying to me. Thankfully, my husband was listening and remembered it all. Roland told me that my mother had always been with me. Throughout the last twenty-five years she was always thinking about me. She had never stopped loving me and she apologized for the abuse I endured as a child. After all these years, and all the sorrow and trauma, she finally believed me about my childhood. This message alone was more than I could handle. The tears were streaming down my face faster than they could be wiped away. I had a large knot in the pit of my stomach, but my heart was soaring. Then Roland gave me one of the greatest gifts I had even received and now one of my most precious possessions . . . a Purple Paper message from my mother!

My Purple Paper had been written the morning of the event. My mother had visited Roland that very morning with a message for me! On the top of the paper were several years: 1986, 1991, 1993, 1998, 2001, and 2010. Roland was unaware of the connection for each year, but I knew. Each year signified a significant occurrence in my life. One year was when my daughter was born, one when my husband and I separated for six months, the birth of my son was another, and one signified when my oldest son graduated from high school. There was absolutely no way Roland could have possibly known any of this information. Along with the years, the message was directed to "my daughter" and spoke about her always being with me and believing in me: "I need to tell my daughter that I'm sorry about how our lives changed. It started out (OK) long ago. I was (almost) always in a bad place. My mind was never settled. You made the right decisions and never forgot it."

9-23-2016 Roland M Comtois - The Purple Papers 1986-1991- 1993
Channeled Messages for 1998. 2001-2010
www.blessingsbyroland.com

I need to tell my daughter
that I'm so sorry about how
our lives changed. It started out
(ok) long ago. I was (almost) always
in a bad place. My mind was never
settled. You made the right decision
and never forget it.

As I left the event with my sacred Purple Paper in my hands, I felt an enormous amount of healing had just occurred for me. I had healed in my grief and in my trauma due to the messages and Purple Paper. I can now see my mother and our relationship in a totally different light and allow myself to let go of the anger toward her and give her love. Because of this event, my life and my history have changed forever.

Chapter 20

MATTHEW'S STORY
BY CINDY HALLER

I have been blessed with several Purple Papers, all of them alive with messages from my son Matthew, who now lives in the spiritual realm. Each Purple Paper is significant, personal and precious, validation of life beyond and boundless, eternally endless love. Many of these papers have Matthew's name written on them, inked into immortality by my son through Roland's gifted hand. Some come with personal messages that only I would understand. Others reveal personal private issues. I have chosen to write about those Purple Paper messages that can be easily validated, in part because I want potential naysayers to say nay no more. Spiritual communications are an important part of life, the very essence of love. I wouldn't want to deny anyone, believer or not, the beauty and bounty of these missives. They are real and are precious testament to the bonds shared and intact between heaven and earth.

This is Matthew's story.

He was born on March 27, 1984. He left this world on April 12, 2007. He was twenty-three years young.

Matthew came into our lives and hearts nine and a half years after our daughter, Jessica, was born. He was our blessing and a joy to our community of friends. In a sense, he was everyone's baby, but especially to his sister. She adored him as he did her. Matthew was blessed with intelligence, good looks, a beautiful smile, and a sense of humor. Unfortunately, he was not given the opportunity to reach all of his potential as he tragically lost his life in his early twenties. We experienced a parent's worst nightmare coming true.

Although this is a difficult story to tell and read, it is important to do so. It is about a life gone too soon.

On April 11, 2007, I returned to Naples, Florida, from Chicago. My husband, Tim, remained in Chicago. Matthew was living with us.

The last time I saw Matthew was that afternoon when he changed into his dress clothes for work. He was riding his motorcycle to work because he had left our car at a friend's house. Our last words to each other went like this:

"Matthew, you know how Dad and I feel about you riding the motorcycle at night," I said.

"Don't worry, Mom. If I go out tonight, I will take the car," he replied.

As I watch him walk out the door, I said, "You can't see yourself from the back, but you look mighty fine."

On April 12, 2007, I was awakened in the middle of the night to the police at our front door. Matthew was shot, they informed me, in our car.

I have lived with the "if only" ever since. "If only Matthew had been on his motorcycle, he could have driven away."

I immediately needed to know that Matthew still existed and was OK. I sought out mediums. Through the messages I have received, I know that while he is no longer alive in the flesh, he is always with me in spirit.

Matthew never lets an opportunity to get a message to me go by, especially through Roland. I am blessed to have eight Purple Paper messages from him, each providing me with reassurance that he continues to be present in our lives.

The Purple Paper dated February 3, 2015, has important validations that our son lives on in spirit:

"Mom, I'll always be your 'smile.'" Matthew was always known for his beautiful, endearing smile. I smiled when I read it and still do.

"When I passed at 23 years old, you (passed) (in your heart) too." He was 23 when he died, and, yes, a huge part of me stopped living that day too.

"I love being near the water with you." Matthew's father and I spend the winters in Florida. On Matthew's angel day, April 12, we go the beach house with his photo. I always wear his blue plaid shirt, and we release blue balloons, his favorite color.

"Sometimes when you're quiet, you can hear me. But, it's really hard for you to get quiet." I often talk with Matthew silently in my thoughts. But it is hard for me to get quiet! So true!

"I'm glad you're still here (earth) and me (heaven) because you are really needed."

My Purple Paper dated June 6, 2016, was brief, but powerful.

It started with "Hey, Mom. It's me, 'Matt,' 'Matty,' 'Matthew.'" I can't express how hearing and seeing these three names touched my heart. Yes, our son was called Matt, Matty, and Matthew by all who knew him. I always called him Matthew.

"I am so alive here. Stop worrying." Yes, I have worried, asking myself again and again, does Matthew still exist? Who is he as a spiritual self? Is he OK?

"I'm still your boy." It is so important to have this reassurance. Over and over, I have cried, "I still want Matthew to be my son," even when I cross over.

My Purple Paper dated January 28, 2017, addressed my persistent concerns about how he passed. Was he scared? Did he suffer?

"Mom, please (from this day forward), don't be in pain about how I passed. I wasn't afraid at all. No pain … no pain … You're strong … You've always been."

Always sensitive to others, he was trying to release me from the worry about how he passed, how he was murdered.

"I'm still your boy with a big smile."

I have pleaded with a broken heart that Matthew is still my son, my boy. And he was always known for his big beautiful smile.

"I was sitting with [you] this first week of October." My birthday is October 7, the first week of October. Knowing that he is there with me on my special day is the best gift I could ever receive.

1-28-2017 I was sitting with
this first week of October
Mom, Please (from this day
forward) don't be in pain about
how I passed. I'm still your boy
with a big smile. I wasn't afraid
at all. NO pain... no pain...
You're strong... you'll always be
PS I always do.

Another special Purple Paper from January 23, 2014, read, "Mom, you always made my life perfect. I will always be your son. I saw the angels near me when I passed. I saw Grandma too. I love you for always trying to make it right for me. Look for the (heart). Matthew."

1-23-2014 Mom, you always made
my life perfect. I
will always be your son.
I saw the angels
near me when I passed.
I saw grandma, too. I
love you for always trying to
make it right for me.
Look for the ♡... Matthew

A second one from the same day showed these meaningful words: "Mom, it's me standing with you when you're home alone. I know every day you ask me to be here…I'm there. I give you HUGS and SMILES all the time. Yes, I watch over my sister…I promise."

Chapter 21

THE THREE JS

BY MARY ANN BLAKELY

My father, who was my hero and larger than life when I was a child, passed away on March 18, 1995. It was very difficult losing him, as he was always my rock. I knew I could count on him for good advice and help whenever I needed it. He was a strong man, an ex-Marine, a police detective, a good provider, and most importantly, a loving and very humorous man. He knew how to tell a great story and was often asked to be toastmaster by friends and acquaintances, who knew he would rise to the occasion. Whenever he spoke, he left everyone holding their sides and crying from laughing. I was the oldest of his five children and everyone said he favored me. That made me so proud.

My father was raised in New Jersey. He was the son of a German immigrant who came to this country as a young boy under his new stepfather's name when his mother remarried. My father was also raised with that surname. His mother died when he was a toddler, and he was passed around to be raised by various family members when his father went off with the Merchant Marines. I do not know when my grandfather died, but it was when my father was a very young man.

My father joined the Marines during World War II. He learned from his aunt what his real surname was and went to the town hall to search for his birth certificate. My grandfather had used the surname on my father's birth certificate because my father was American born and in no danger of being deported. Right then and there, my father decided to use that surname as his own from then on.

Off my father went into the Marine Corps. Like so many young men in those days, he married a local girl right before he was shipped off to the South Pacific. After the war, he returned to New Jersey and to his war bride. They tried to make a go of it, but things did not work out. They divorced while their baby was still an infant.

My father left New Jersey and moved to Connecticut, where he met and courted my mother. They fell in love, married, and had five children together during their happy forty-eight-year marriage.

Dad never shared with us the fact that he had been married before or that he had a son by his first wife. When she remarried, her new husband wanted to raise the boy with his surname as they had other children. So when the boy was just six years old, my dad went back to New Jersey to sign off on the adoption papers and relinquish all rights to his firstborn son.

We all lived our lives without any knowledge of this until three months after my father died. That's when we heard from his son, Jack. It was June 1995. Apparently, his adopted father had just passed away, and his mother was now free to divulge who Jack's biological father was. Even though our father had passed away too, we agreed to meet this man. He was now living close by in Long Island.

It was a beautiful reunion. Here was a man who so greatly resembled my father, both in appearance and in his gregarious, outgoing personality. We bonded instantly with a bear hug. It was love at first sight, and I immediately adored my big brother.

Here's the missing piece of the puzzle. I had secretly known about him since I was thirteen after reading a document that had been left out on Dad's dresser. My mother made me promise never to speak of it. It was my father's secret to tell. I kept that promise close to my heart, always wondering about the little boy who was named after my dad.

For the next six years, my big brother and I made up for lost time. We were very close. We spoke frequently on the phone. He called me "sis." We visited each other's homes, often staying overnight. We went on outings and attended each other's birthday parties. He was like a "soul twin" to me. Unfortunately, my siblings did not share this strong familial bond. They never got to know Jack like I did. When he died on September 6, 2001, from liver cancer, just six years after he came into my life, I was devastated and grief stricken. It was like losing my dad all over again.

After my brother Jack died, I wondered if he was with my dad. Did they find each other after the both died? Did my dad meet up with his own mother and father? Would they even know each other? My grandfather, father, and his son all grew up with three different surnames, but they all originally had the same exact names, first, middle, and last.

On September 29, 2006, I went to see Roland at a Channeled Messages for the Soul event. I brought my journal with me, along with three pictures I kept inside. One was of my grandfather, one was of my father, and the other one was of my brother Jack.

I sat in the audience of about forty people wearing nametags with their first names, hoping that Roland would have a message for me. He came into the room, introduced himself, and began telling his story. Then he quieted down and became still. He started to single out different people, speaking to them intimately about loved ones who had passed. Of course, the tissues started to be passed around. Then Roland came up to me, stopped, and looked me right in the eye. He said excitedly, "You are surrounded by love, Mary Anne. There's a man standing next to you, not old. There's a youthfulness about him. There are three men in the same family. Your brother is here … Your father is here … Your grandfather is here. Your father says he loves his little girl … he's talking about love … a soul mate. He says, sorrows will ease, a peace will come. You've been having headaches. They are working on you. You will be more at ease. A soul mate … pray. Stay true to your truth. Somebody left you. You fell in love … he's coming back."

Roland stopped and just looked at me like a light bulb just went off. He headed to the table in front of the room and started to rifle through a stack of Purple Papers. "I know it's here. I know it's for you. Can you believe it?"

Suddenly, he returned with a large Purple Paper dated September 25 written four days earlier with a black marker.

The message said, "All three are gone. All three have the same 1st name." Yes, they are all named John. "Picture of all three." I opened my journal and showed Roland the three pictures. Then, inside a circle that was drawn on the paper was written "son, father, grandfather." Yes, that is their relationship to one another. Then Roland turned the paper over to reveal the words "3 men from one family will gather to speak to the little girl."

Tears of joy streamed down my face. They were all together, and they are still with me. It was the most awesome, fulfilling, amazing spiritual feeling of my life.

I have been to see Roland at other events since then, always hoping for another message. On one such occasion, at the end I went up to ask Roland a question. I asked if my daughter who had been married for six years and was trying for a child would ever make me a grandmother. He said yes but the problem wasn't hers. It was her husband's, on his left side. I told my daughter what Roland said and her husband went to the doctor's to be checked out. It turned out that Roland was right, and the problem was solved. My first grandchild was a boy, and my daughter named him after my brother Jack. He was born on June 7, 2009. I was with him the moment he was born. We locked eyes and the love connection was immediate and strong. I remain very close to that little boy Jack.

I went to see Roland again on October 16, 2009. He had a Purple Paper for me, dated October 13, 2009. This one only had three words written on it: "Jack is free!!!"

I feel my grandson Jack has so much of his Great Uncle Jack in him and also his great grandfather. Having him is a blessing and a comfort.

Chapter 22

ROSE'S GIFT

BY KAREN PAGANO

I have always known that I was adopted and have always wondered about my history. I began my search for answers more than twenty years ago, but after being thwarted by sealed records and falsified information, I was reluctant to go on another quest and face failure and rejection once again.

But that didn't stop me from constantly wondering about the circumstances that caused my birth parents to give me up. Why did they choose to send me out to the world alone? Were there regrets and repercussions? Did that decision free them from a responsibility they were not ready to assume? Or was my mother alone, confused, and afraid? Was the choice forced upon her by a society that frowned upon out-of-wedlock births? Did she make a sacrifice to give me a chance at a better life?

As my fiftieth birthday approached and I faced this milestone year, I was still wrestling with these unanswered questions. I had just signed up to attend a channeling event and for some reason, I felt the tug of certainty pull hard at my heart. Was I about to find the answers I sought for decades?

It was my first time at an event like this. I brought along one of my bronzed baby shoes, having been told that carrying a cherished item could open the doors to the other side and make communication easier. The shoe would prove to be the catalyst I had been searching for. The missing link I had been carrying with me for decades.

The bronzed baby shoe is one of those marvels. How was it a link in the chain of events that led me to my family? The shoe was bronzed at the local "shoe hospital" that my adoptive father and I would visit as we did our weekend chores when I was a child. In those days, our shoes were repaired and resoled until we outgrew them, so we visited it often. I remember the excursions to the repair shop very well: the high counters and the special platform for the policemen to sit and have their boots shined. I remember my adoptive father and the shop owner, an animated Italian, talking at length about the news of the day. I remember the train set, occasionally set up in a corner, and the little boy sitting transfixed by its sound and motion.

I had no specific expectations for the event other than to learn about mediumship and the form it might take in my life. I did believe in spiritual communications and the transformative power of intention, and I knew that it was time to allow myself the experience.

The space was dimly lit, cozy and warm. A group of twenty-five or so was seated in quiet expectation. Soft music played as Roland entered the room. He turned to face us and said softly, "The energy is changing, there are angels around us. Who has that baby shoe?" I sat in amazement but felt no impulse to respond, nor did Roland wait for an answer. I knew he was talking to me and that this was the beginning of an important journey.

Lost family members and friends from the other side had messages for most of the people in the room, and the time rolled smoothly and safely along. I did not receive a message for any person I had lost, but Roland did tell me that my dog, Ditto, was sitting beside me. It was so comforting to know that she was still at my side and offering her love and protection. As the night ended, I sat bathed in a glow of newly felt possibility and promise. Roland announced that he would be holding individual sessions over the weekend, so I signed up to meet with him the following day.

Roland was sitting quietly when I entered the room for my private session and asked if I had any special items with me. I put the baby shoe on the table and he began. He was receiving messages from two men, one of them a father, offering me support and guidance. He began to give me information about my birth: I was born at a home for unwed mothers at 11:33 p.m. after my mother was transported from a bar by two male friends. I was small and refused to breathe when I entered the world. I was taken to another room, where I was stabilized. My mother did not see or touch me. I would never breathe air in the same room as the woman who gave birth to me. My life in the orphanage was about to begin.

A young novitiate, seventeen-year-old Sister Mary Frances, would be my savior. She took a special interest in me and fed and comforted me, helping me grow strong and healthy over the next three months. I was soon adopted and given a new life, full of love, support, and opportunities I would not have otherwise known.

The session was ending, and Roland suddenly stood up and said, "I have a Purple Paper for you. It is from your mother, Rose." The message was simple and poignant: "[She] will need to know we still love her." He handed it to me, and I asked if I should keep on searching.

"Yes," he said. "You must start today!" A wound had been opened in my heart that had not had proper healing, and I knew that I was starting a new course of treatment with this knowledge. I found comfort in knowing that my mother had offered the connection through the Purple Paper.

I did continue to search that day. I knew my original last name because of an error made at a town office years before when I was mistakenly given a copy of my original birth certificate. Before submitting it at a passport office, I opened the form and saw the name I was given at birth. After seeing Roland, I contacted an online adoptee search agency, and within hours they found my birth mother's oldest brother. I was able to find him at a retirement home and told him I was the daughter of his youngest sister, Rose. I was amazed to see a man who looked very much like me. We had the same hair and skin color, similar blue eyes and face shape. I knew this man was my uncle.

He offered to call a nephew, my cousin, who may have remembered Rose being pregnant with me. I was contacted within days and given the information I needed. My cousin told me that my mother had lived with them while she was pregnant and had a son five years later by my birth father. They had married. He had the contact information for my brother, Michael.

The news that I had a full birth brother was both shocking and unsettling, but I was determined to attempt a connection. I tried to contact him, first by a telephone call and a year later with a Christmas card. Neither approach resulted in a response. I decided to wait and allow time for him and me to absorb the reality of being siblings. After a few more years, I decided to do a drive by to see where my brother was living. Needless to say, I found myself struggling with whether or not to invade his privacy. I struggled with the steering wheel too and found myself turning into the yard and "driving" into Michael's life.

I was greeted by a woman who took a quick look at me and said, "You do not have to tell me who you are. You look just like your mother—and your brother has had the card that you sent him on his bureau ever since he got it." My sister-in-law told me what she knew about my mother, that she struggled with depression and alcoholism throughout her life and had raised Michael alone after a very short marriage with my father, Victor. Life had been hard for Rose and Michael, but they stayed in touch after he married and he visited occasionally.

Rose was kind and quiet in her later years and had passed nearly ten years earlier. She had never spoken of me, although my brother did know of my existence. He had invited our father to visit from California to celebrate the birth of Michael's first child, a son. Sworn to secrecy, he was told that he had an older sister who was given up at birth. Sadly, Victor died soon after the revelation, and my brother was left knowing only that I existed, but with no way to find me, as my birth records remain closed to this day.

I did meet my brother that day. The first thing that he asked me was if I ever felt abandoned. I replied that I was, so I did. He answered that he too felt abandoned, even though he lived with our mother growing up. That feeling was one of our first common bonds. We shared other things too: a quick wit, a love of music and reading, high cholesterol, and other physical traits. We both struggled with depression, which he tried to ease with alcohol, as did our mother.

We began an easy relationship, with occasional visits and planned family events. We enjoyed our talks together, although Michael did not talk about life with our mother, Rose. I understood and accepted that it was painful and a reminder of a tough time in his life. I was not to know more about the woman who gave me the gift of life.

Michael died unexpectedly after I had known him for just a few years. It was a new kind of sadness for me, losing someone who was emotionally and biologically connected to me. I am so grateful that the birth of my nephew brought our father back to share the secret of my birth. I often wonder if I would have been allowed into Michael's life if he had not known about me. Would he have kept the Christmas card for all those years and warmly welcomed me as he did on the day of our first meeting? I was also blessed to remain a part of Michael's family. I continue to share special occasions with them and look forward to watching his wife and children, now young adults, make their way in the world. I marvel at the mystery, miracles, and magic sent by family and friends now passed.

What I discovered when I found my brother and learned the identity of my parents was that the man who owned the repair shop and bronzed my baby shoe was actually my birth father, Victor. And the boy who sometimes visited with his train set was my brother, Michael. And none of us knew of our connections to one another. The circle, like the toy train's circuitous path, is now complete.

I have received the gift of my mother Rose with humble heart and awe-inspired appreciation. And I await more revelations to come in those precious Purple Papers!

Chapter 23

A SECOND CHANCE

BY ROXANNE JASPARRO

Dad had his first heart attack when I was sixteen years old. A year later he had another one. It was fatal. Both happened when he was on the porch that led into the sunroom.

I had been a typical teenager with a mind of my own when my father experienced his first heart attack. Like so many kids my age, I was rebellious and thwarted his attempts at conversation and camaraderie. Truth be told, we were on the "outs" then. His heart attack was a wake-up call and, in a funny sort of way, brought us closer together. Gratefully, we were given a second chance to rekindle that father-daughter relationship we once had cherished, and we made the most of it. We spent that next year talking, laughing, learning about each other, reconnecting, and loving our time together. Looking back on it now, I can honestly say it was one of the happiest years of my childhood.

Then it happened again. My father had a massive heart attack that proved fatal. I was seventeen. The paramedics who answered the call that day did all they could to save him, but my father passed away quickly.

Many years later and just a few years after my wedding, I visited the set of Roland's radio show, *Soul Stories*. My aunt Diane was his cohost, and I loved the show. Being an intuitive medium myself, I too get messages. During that first show, every time I was near Roland, I would get the same message over and over again. I kept hearing, "I have something to tell you." I kept thinking I had something to tell Roland but couldn't figure out the message! I told my aunt that I had something to tell him but didn't know what it was. It was a struggle at this point because I had suppressed my childhood gift after my father's death, but that phrase just kept repeating itself to the point of total frustration.

It was when I went to Roland's Purple Paper page on Facebook to view the papers posted for that night's radio show that I received the rest of my message! Roland displayed ten Purple Papers for that night's show and then slipped in an extra one that ended up being meant for me. It was the story of my dad's passing and read, "I had a heart attack at the front door. It was so quick that I didn't feel sick. I am peaceful now. (Yes, I am peaceful now.)"

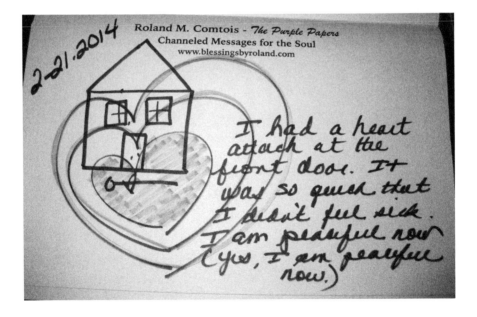

The voice in my head got stronger when I saw the Purple Paper message. I still heard, "I have something to tell you." I thought I had a message for Roland, and I thought my dad was trying to navigate the whole situation.

Not being able to physically go to the radio station, I called in. Luckily, I got through, still thinking I was going to have this big important message to give to Roland because the words in my head, "I have something to tell you," kept getting stronger. I asked Roland about the Purple Paper I saw on Facebook, waiting for guidance on the message I would give to him, and instead Roland said to me, "I have something to tell you. I have been here all along. Be patient. Slow down. I'm happy. I'm at peace."

The voice in my head was my dad! It was not a message for Roland but a message from my dad *through* Roland! I got the message, and from that point on, my intuitive gifts continued to open up and bless my life in meaningful ways.

Chapter 24

LOOK FOR THE DIMES

BY WENDY M. KARSPECK

I had seen Roland several times, but my friend was new to the experience. I prepared her as best you can when you are explaining that there really are people who can talk with the departed and who spend their time sharing messages from ones who passed into another realm. But I think you have to experience it for yourself before you really truly can wrap your head around it.

This one particular night, we were sitting among the other attendees when Roland came up to me and started talking about my grandmother. He said, "She sent you the blue jays." My friend's jaw dropped, because the weekend before we went to see Roland, I was on the phone with her while sitting on my deck and noted, "There are at least fifteen blue jays in my backyard. I haven't seen a blue jay in five years."

The next time I went to see Roland, I was completely stunned by a statement he wrote on the Purple Paper message he gave me. My dad died in March 2015, and I went to see Roland in September of that same year. I had no expectations then, probably out of fear of being disappointed if my dad didn't come through. But he did come through, and so did my nephew who died in a tragic car accident at the age of twenty-four.

Roland asked his assistant to find the Purple Paper about the car accident. Then he turned back to me and said, "Your father will leave you three dimes in thirty-five days." I found this statement to be so specific and odd at the same time. At the end of the night, when Roland handed out the Purple Paper messages, I anxiously waited for mine about the car accident. But Roland didn't give it to me.

Confused, I asked his assistant before I left if she had it. She said, "Yes, but Roland has to give it to you." He asked me a lot of questions before he handed over the paper. It was apparent to me that Roland wants to give the right messages to the people they are meant for, so he took great care to ascertain that this was my message. I felt every hair on my body stand up as I read the message from my nephew: "The car accident was an accident. I did get distracted (a little bit) but never saw the tree. When the accident happened, I passed away immediately."

But it was the last line of his message that really got to me. It stated, "Look for the dimes."

Roland M. Comtois - *The Purple Papers*
Channeled Messages for the Soul
www.blessingsbyroland.com

8.11.2015

The car accident, was an accident. I did get distracted (a little bit), but never saw the tree. When the accident happened I passed away immediately. Look for the dimes......

This confirmed to me that our loved ones want us to know they are still with us and they send us various signs to validate this fact. The paper was dated August 11, 2015 (before I even purchased my ticket to the event), and it let me know that my nephew and father are together in heaven—conspiring.

On the thirty-fifth day, I was getting frustrated because everyone who had heard about the Purple Paper message was texting me about the dimes they found, but I still hadn't found one single dime. That night my roommate and I were arguing over who should do the dishes. I won the argument. When my roommate ran the garbage disposal after finishing the dishes, there was an awful noise. He reached down the disposal to see what had caused it. To our surprise, he found a dime and two pennies. Now, how does change get into a garbage disposal?

The next day I found two more dimes, adding up to the three dimes my father had promised me in the Purple Paper message. I find dimes all the time now, and each time I do, I think of my father.

My favorite time was on February 5, 2016, my dad's first birthday in heaven. We had a nor'easter and I was stuck in the house crying all day. I finally mustered up the energy to shovel my way out of the storm. The snow was extremely heavy, so after finishing clearing the walkway, I decided to take a break before I tackled the driveway. I was only in the house for about ten minutes before I headed out again. And there directly in the middle of the pathway I had just shoveled was the shiniest dime I have ever seen! There is no possible way it was there before. I would have shoveled it into oblivion, and I remember actually scraping ice from that portion of the walkway. There had been no dime there before I went into the house. My mood immediately brightened, as I knew my dad left that dime there to let me know how much I am loved and missed.

Chapter 25

MY MOM

BY TARA GERVAIS

What does one say about one's mother? Beyond the realm of anger and resentment, the what ifs and I should haves, when one's relationship to one's parent is fruitful, loving, and openly honest, all that a child could hope for is really and truly only love, admiration, and a friendship that stands head and shoulders above all others. Of course, there is hardship along the way: arguments that became shouting matches of dueling wills, misunderstandings that seemed unbridgeable, and the crushing tension of unbridled youth butting up against weathered experience. But sometimes the good outweighs the bad, and you forget about the tough times. That is, until the really tough times come beating down your door and hold a knife to the throat of your entire life.

Like too many others, cancer affected my family in the most grievous of ways: it took my mother away from us and tore a hole in my universe. She was the most important person in my life, and not a day goes by that I don't mourn her loss, even while I try to cope and live by her light. Some feelings you never "get over." You just learn to live with them. I know a lot of people out there know exactly how I feel.

For eighteen years, my darling Debra, mom to me and my brother, valiant defender of us both, suffered from the scourge of breast cancer. Radiation, chemotherapy, experimental drugs, reconstructive surgery—you name it, we tried it. There were successes and failures along the way, and for several years, through strife and pain and, above all, hope, we held on to her. She stayed strong enough to live and thrive, and yet we knew we were dodging bullets. She was forever weakened, and we knew anytime there could come a day where the scans came back positive or there was another lump, and our time together could suddenly become unavoidably limited. Then six years ago, she was diagnosed as terminal, with five years to live. And exactly five years and two months later, on January 7, 2017, we said our final goodbyes. She'd put herself through so much for the love of her family; she wouldn't give up, she'd said, because she had so much to live for. But enough was enough, and we couldn't watch her fading away and falling apart. Once we gave her our blessing, it wasn't long after that she left this world, bound for a place without pain and fear, and went all the way up to heaven.

My mom was a very bright woman. She was full of smiles and laughter and rarely met anyone who didn't immediately adore her. During her sixty-one years on this earth, and especially in the wake of her passing, so many people would go on and on about how much of a mother figure she had been in their lives. Coworkers, friends, extended family, and even my own friends were very vocal about their love for her, her generous spirit, the kindness of her face, and her limitless counsel when something needed to be figured out. So many of their anecdotes were so poignant, and my brother and I were moved and smiled at the thought of so many people seeing in her exactly what we'd always known was her essence: a beautiful soul and an understanding heart. She was cremated as she had requested, and her memorial service was filled with stories about her, both funny and sad, while we played her favorite music on the speakers. No pipe organ or silence for our Deb, just Fleetwood Mac and Led Zeppelin, as she no doubt would have preferred.

The "firsts" after a loved one's passing are always the hardest. The holidays would be doubly hard for us as her swift decline in health began on Thanksgiving night around the dessert table, when she lost her words and became shaky and disoriented, because the dozens of tiny tumors in her brain had finally gotten a foothold, unbeknownst to anyone. My birthday is the beginning of summer, and I dreaded it without her. Mom had a tradition of calling people on their birthday, and, whether you picked up or she got your machine, she sang "Happy Birthday" off key and adorably. She had become known for it among her close friends and family. The thought of never again getting that phone call filled me with sorrow and bore a hole into my gut. Needless to say, I wasn't looking forward to it at all.

On the very day of my birthday, my cousin Lisa was watching one of Roland's live feeds on Facebook. He was reading many of his Purple Papers aloud and showed them to his viewers. The very first one was from a woman named Debbie: "Debbie says that the 5 weeks before she passed were really hard. But before that, I wasn't too bad. The 'drugs' weren't doing the job. My body was resistant to many things. I [am] happy to say my pain is really gone." She wanted her loved ones to know she was finally out of pain.

6-27-2017 Roland M. Comtois - *The Purple Papers*
www.RolandComtois.net

Debbie says that the 5 weeks before she passed were really hard. But before that, I wasn't too bad. The "drugs" weren't doing the job. My body was resistant to many things. I happy to say, my pain is really gone.

Lisa sent me the link and when I saw it for myself, I wept openly, stirred to my bones at the accuracy of it all. Her last five weeks were filled with radiation and pills that never seemed to work, and the situation became what we had most feared but knew would one day happen. Further along in the video, Roland, while communing with the spirits, stopped talking at one point and called out my mother's name, and then Lisa's. "Lisa, your cousin Debbie wants you to know she's OK. You guys used to be so close and she's sorry you fell out of touch. 'I love you, Lisa,' she's saying. But this message isn't for you; it's for her daughter on her birthday. 'Happy birthday, my girl.'"

Every time I think of that video my skin goes to goosebumps and my eyes brim with tears. I needed her so much every day since her passing, but especially on that day. And there she was, pushing through the static and the space between worlds to let me know that she was still there with me, watching over with concern and love, no doubt hoping my brother and I could find the strength to soldier on without her. I had felt so lost without that song on my telephone, and when Roland spoke, I could hear her voice again. The comfort it gave me I cannot measure in any real way other than by how much it soothed my heart. Before my mom's passing, I had been skeptical of the afterlife, always a realist who needed proof of everything. She, however, had always been very spiritual, and never wavered from her belief that death was not the end and that love could transcend all boundaries. This was all the proof anyone could need, and I again felt her presence wash over me as she wished me a happy birthday.

About six months later, we went to see Roland in person in his hometown of Woonsocket, Rhode Island, where we had all been born and lived so much of our lives, my mother especially. That was the night my brother received his message. Roland approached him at our table, leaned into his face, and said, "I am so proud of you. The man you've become is more than I ever could have hoped. You never disappointed me or disturbed me. I know we didn't have enough time together, but what we had was so great. I'm always here." Roland put his hand on my brother's shoulder and said, "There is always love around you." My brother cried and cried, feeling what I had felt: her presence, her love once again, that wave of relief and bittersweet feeling that I had felt on my birthday. My brother at that point in time was having a hard time coping with the coming holidays and the void she had left behind that would never be filled. She reached out to me when I needed her most, and she did the same for him. We approached Roland that evening with our story, and here we are, forever grateful for our messages, healing slowly but surely, and remembering her strength in life so that we might find a bit of our own to live on.

I just wish there was a way to reply, to tell her thank you, for being an incredible mother, for loving us unconditionally, for never letting us feel like we were anything less than treasures to her, for putting herself through hell to stay with us for so many years. Our whole family was around her that snowy day in January when she took her last breaths and became our angel. We were lucky enough to have had time with her before the end, and my brother and I were in fact able to say all those things. But we can't help but wish for one more conversation, one more joke, one more hug, and to be able to express our gratitude just one more time. But then I remember that she's always with me, so I say it all out loud, and I know, wherever she is, finally free of pain and watching us live by her light, she hears me.

Chapter 26

SORRY

BY KERRI GERRARD

Someone I know read a Purple Paper posted on Facebook and messaged me. "I think this message is for you," she said.

It read, "I know that how I passed causes you such pain. I'm sorry. I'm sorry. I'm sorry. I'm sorry. I'm sorry. Mom, you *could not* have known. You're a good mom to me. (Sit and pray.)"

I immediately logged on to Roland's page to get a closer look. I knew it was for me the minute I read it. It was dated June 1, 2014, six months after my son, Dan, took his own life in the early morning hours of January 3. My son tattooed "sorry" on his chest a couple of years before he died. The desk depicted in the upper left corner of the Purple Paper with "stuff" on it is very meaningful. This is where my son left all of his personal belongings in a manila envelope and in a small box that said "sorry" on it. He left a suicide note, his special ring, his Social Security card, and a picture ID on his desk. He had just gotten that desk and was so excited when it was given to him.

Roland M. Comtois - *The Purple Papers*
Channeled Messages for the Soul
www.blessingsbyroland.com

I know that how I passed causes you such pain. I'm sorry. I'm sorry. I'm sorry. I'm so sorry.

I'm Sorry.

mom. you could not have known. you're a good mom to (sit and me. play)

He stated in the note that to spare us any further pain, we could find him in the water under the Henderson Bridge in East Providence, Rhode Island. He jumped. Because of the winter conditions that year, his body was not found until June 19, 2014. He was found under the Brown University boat dock. Again, I knew in my heart my son wanted to somehow alleviate my pain by leaving me this message. In my wildest dreams I would never have thought my son would have taken his own life. So, I had reached out to Roland and said I know this Purple Paper is mine. He determined months later that it was.

My son, Daniel, was twenty years old when he took his own life. He was funny and had many friends. He was the family comedian. He was a talented artist and hip-hop emcee. He was a writer. He was beyond creative and smart. He had a high IQ and was wise beyond his years. He loved books, art, and music. He did spot-on impressions of celebrities, including Dr. Phil, John Travolta as his character in *Grease*, and Christopher Walken. He would give a homeless person his last five dollars. He was an avid skateboarder. He loved conspiracy theories and deep debates on any subject. He very rarely watched television, but he did have some favorite shows, *Dexter*, *Shameless*, *Weeds*, and *Breaking Bad* among them. My son was the youngest of my children. He had two older sisters who adored him and miss him dearly. He was the glue that always held us together. He never held a grudge and was polite and friendly. He was everything I hoped for and more than I can describe. He was beyond beautiful and is now beyond the pain that caused him to take his life.

I last saw my son on Christmas Day 2013. He didn't talk about his feelings and was always happy, or so we thought. When I received a second Purple Paper message, it was clear that my son wanted me to know it was not my fault and that it was his mind that got the best of him. Here's what it said:

"Mom, I know you tried to find me the minute I was gone. I drifted away (in my mind), not from you. I spent some time in my life trying to find peace. I'm glad you found me. I am so safe in heaven. I'll always be there (in your heart)."

10-18-2016 Roland M. Comtois - *The Purple Papers*
Channeled Messages for the Soul
www.blessingsbyroland.com

Mom, I know you tried to find me the minute I was gone. I drifted away (in my mind), not from you. I spent some time, in my life, trying to find peace. I'm glad you found me. I am so safe in Heaven. I'll always be there (in your head.)

Roland gave me that message in person when I attended one of his events. As Roland was speaking, he described feeling cold and wet. He delivered the first part of the message with a lot of enthusiasm and animation, like my son did when he was excited. Then Roland grabbed me by the shoulders and looked directly into my eyes. He was in my personal space, which is how Dan always addressed me when he wanted my full attention. Roland said, "Your son wants you to know none of this is your fault and you could not have known." Then he also said that I was his hero and that he comes to me at night.

He thanked people for comforting me during the message. He made himself known, as he had always done. Roland kept coming back to me during the two-hour event because Dan kept hounding him to reiterate what he wanted to say in the matter-of-fact way Dan always spoke. When he handed me the Purple Paper, Roland was very somber and down and with a lot of sadness. I have no doubt my son was trying to alleviate my pain and sadness, and I'm so thankful for Roland delivering it to me.

My son did not believe in God, but yet says he's safe in heaven. I'm happy he's safe there. I was a believer in spiritual communications even before the Purple Papers. His letter said he's not sure where he would end up or start again, but I know he believes in life after death now and is making the most of it.

Chapter 27

HEAVEN ON EARTH

BY JOAN DIMAIO

Of the six Purple Papers I received, the first three Purple Papers were channeled at an event in 2011. It was the first time I had met Roland in person. I had been listening to his *Soul Stories* broadcast on the radio for a while and when I heard he was going to be promoting his book *And Then There Was Heaven* near my home, I made plans to be there.

I felt it was a golden opportunity to finally meet him in person. I purchased his book, listened to him talk about his journey, and then waited at the table to have my book signed. Little did I know he would channel a message from my mom. I have to be honest with you, because back then Roland drew quickly and talked fast. I was overwhelmed with emotions when I gazed at the Purple Papers. It took me a while to process it all. The amazing thing about this paper was the fact he knew my name and the X on the paper was exactly where I sat as my mom was passing. It said, "Joan, you had to [let] me go. You had no more choices. No control, no choices." How could he have possibly known this? How could he possibly know that there were no more choices? I had to let her go. I tried so hard to help her, and sadly I had to tell her to go.

How poignant it was to see that Roland wrote another message from my mother saying, "I'm still your angel." I just love that! "Setting me free, you did right by me."

My journey to healing began that day.

The next paper, dated October 18, 2013, was from my dad, who curiously had passed away in the same month some six years earlier. On it he said he loved me: "Mom was waiting for me. I wasn't afraid. I love you." My dad never told me he loved me while he lived on this earth, so to see that written on the paper was very special to me. "Tell my daughter that when I was passing, I saw your mother. Her skin was very beautiful (and pink). You know how much I missed her, right?" The words "pink lipstick" were added to the picture. That was mom, always with the lipstick and rouge on—so cool Roland knew that. They are together now and at peace.

On the Purple Paper dated March 10, 2014, three hearts painted a poignant scene. Mom and Dad passed three years apart, as noted on the paper ("3 years later"), and a stick figure to the left of their beds was me sitting by their sides both times. The message on this paper was again from my dad, who said, "Our daughter took such good care of us. Mom was the first to go, and you know how brokenhearted I was. I was glad it was my time." It is amazing to see how their love for me lives on. It is validating that Roland not only knew about the details surrounding their deaths but that he channeled messages in specific months that were significant to my parents and me. My father began to get sick in the month of March when Roland drew him lying in a bed, just a few months after Mom passed away. He died three years later, exactly as was written on the Purple Paper.

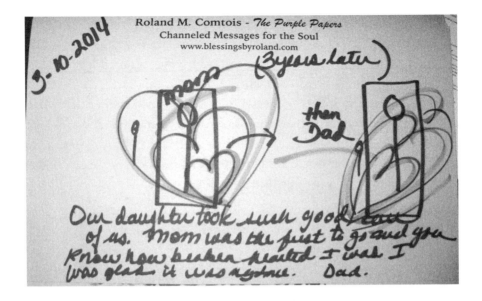

Purple Paper number four blossoms with joy. Dated December 18, 2014, the same month of my mother's passing ten years earlier, it depicted flowers in yellow, pink, and green. How my mother loved her flower garden! Roland wrote, "Katherine remembers days of tending to the garden. I loved spring when the flowers started to come. I couldn't wait to see all the flowers. I found that same place in heaven. It is so beautiful here."

Roland gave me a glimpse of her heaven on that Purple Paper.

I still miss my parents very much. I miss their physical presence and the beautiful times we shared together. But Roland did teach me over the past years, as I listened to his radio show and attended his events, that they are still with me, their love never dies, their souls live on, and heaven is right here on earth.

Chapter 28

YOU ARE NOT BROKEN
BY KATHI ROBBINS

I was raised Catholic but never agreed with everything I was taught in parochial school. I struggled with what my beliefs were for many, many years and eventually gave up and considered myself an atheist. Then I started reading books about psychic mediums and the afterlife and everything I was reading started to make sense to me. It was as if everything I had ever thought or believed was written on the pages I was reading. That is when I found my spirituality. A large part of that was my strong belief in the afterlife and in the people who were able to communicate with souls who had crossed over. Roland is one of them.

I first met Roland a year or so after my father passed away in 2000. I was blessed to have a private reading with him and received many personal messages from my father that I needed to hear. The next time I was able to spend time with Roland was three years later. He hosted a two-day seminar on the weekend after the tragic Station nightclub fire that took so many young lives in West Warwick, Rhode Island, on February 20, 2003. It was an amazing experience that further strengthened my belief in the afterlife and spiritual communications.

I didn't have the opportunity to see Roland again until October 1, 2017, when I went to his Validating the Afterlife event. It was there that I received two of his amazing Purple Papers. At that time, my life had crashed to the lowest point I had ever been at. I needed Roland and his gift desperately and I came to the event with fear of what would I do if I did not get a message. So much was riding on this day, and although I believe in the afterlife and I fully believe in Roland's gifts, I was terrified of what was going to come.

In the prior two years before this event, my poodle Izzy—my baby girl—had died in my arms. Three weeks later, my best friend passed away from scleroderma at a young age. Four months later, I sat and held my father-in-law's hand while he passed away from Alzheimer's disease at his home on hospice care. A month later my mother was diagnosed with non-small cell lung carcinoma. She was beginning radiation and chemotherapy and was given a prognosis of another year to two years. The treatment was getting more difficult for her to cope with, so I drove down to Florida from Connecticut with my new baby Chloe, a Morkie, who was less than a year old at the time, so that I could help my mom get through her debilitating treatments.

The doctors had told my mom that with treatment, they could "buy" her another year. My mom decided to do it, but warned that if the cancer came back, which was likely, she would not repeat treatment. I told her I didn't blame her and that would have been my decision as well. My mom was undergoing radiation and chemotherapy simultaneously. She completed her radiation but became very ill from the chemotherapy treatment. I was there to care for her, but after two months, she ended up in the hospital. She passed away unexpectedly a week and a half later.

The whole experience of caring for my mother and being with her when she passed away was very bittersweet. We had not had a very good relationship for many years. When she became ill, I offered to care for her mainly because I had a more flexible schedule than my siblings did. I was on disability, so I could be with her as long as she needed me. But beyond that, I had decided that I needed to go to her because it's what I needed to do. I did not want to have any regrets when she was gone. It wasn't that I felt obligated to help her; rather, it was what I needed to do for me. I say that the experience was bittersweet because I wanted to make new memories with my mom to replace some of the negative memories I had. We did just that! Although it was never said, I could tell my mom had regrets for some of the things that happened between us in the past.

We put all that aside and we truly enjoyed each other's company during the short time we had together, and I was able to see a side of her that she would not show to anyone before.

After getting through the services and cleaning out her house after she passed, Chloe and I headed back to Connecticut. Two weeks after I returned, I had to put another dog, Louie, to sleep. He was going to be sixteen years old and his body was just giving out on him. Shortly after that, my godfather passed away. The amount of loss that I had suffered in two years was just astronomical. For the next eight months, I just existed—barely.

I am on disability for fibromyalgia and major depression. My depression had gotten so bad that I didn't know what to do to help myself anymore. I finally went to a new doctor and went through a new treatment called transcranial magnetic stimulation (TMS), a noninvasive procedure that uses magnetic fields to stimulate nerve cells in the brain to improve symptoms of depression. It was a seven-week treatment, and I wasn't seeing the positive results as much as I had hoped.

It was around that time that I signed up to go to another one of Roland's events. I really needed to receive some messages from my mother. I had run out of the money from my inheritance and was very upset with myself because that was supposed to be money to help get me through the rest of my life, but I had to use it for basic living expenses. I received another piece of devastating news and I was at my low point. I bottomed out and I just didn't know what to do anymore. So I truly felt like my life was riding on any message I could receive from Roland that day. Not too much pressure on him!

For a week before the event, I kept talking to my mom and asking her to please come and give me a message. I just kept apologizing to her for spending the money and begged her to forgive me.

I arrived at the event an hour early and got a front row seat! When Roland came out, he immediately started to give messages to a woman who was sitting next to me. Right after speaking to her, he came to me with a Purple Paper he had written that morning. It said, "Tell my daughter that her life is going to get better. I know the last year has been filled with difficult obstacles.

You deserve much more. You deserve happiness. I'm not here to talk about me. I'm here (angels too). We're here to help you. Look for the dragonfly."

10-1-2017 Roland M. Comtois - The Purple Papers
www.RolandComtois.net

Tell my daughter that her life is going to get better. I know the last year has been filled with difficult obstacles. You deserve much more. You deserve happiness. I'm not here to talk about me. I'm here (angels, too) and we're here to help you. Look for the dragonfly.

Roland had drawn a purple dragonfly on the page. I just broke down and sobbed. I was wearing a purple dragonfly necklace because ever since my dad had passed away, he always comes to me in the form of a dragonfly. I actually cried harder when he said that she said she was not there to talk about herself. My mother was a bit of a narcissist and one of our issues was that she would put the spotlight on herself even when I needed it on me, so that part of the message was so important to me.

Roland came and put his hand on my shoulder to comfort me and I could feel my mother's presence so strongly. He told me that my mom said that it was time for change in my life and that I would feel alive again. She then said, "Don't let anyone get the best of you anymore. Don't let anyone get the best of you." He also told me that my mother was pushing me through these very difficult times so that I could have my own life. She said it's the first time I will ever have my own life because I have spent my whole life taking care of other people. He stopped for a moment and just stared as if he were listening and then he said, "You are not broken; there is nothing broken in you." That was something I was continuously asking my mother as I spoke out loud to her. I would always ask her, "What is wrong with me?"

As Roland went on, he picked up his pile of Purple Papers and began reading some. At one point, he just said, "Here is one from Shirley, who was in pain." I didn't think it could be possible, but at the break I went up to the desk where his papers were and asked the woman who was sitting there with Roland if she could find the paper about Shirley. She did. I read it and told her I think it was from my dad, Shirley. When my dad was born, Shirley was a boy's name. It wasn't until Shirley Temple came along that it became a girl's name. After I explained this to the woman who was holding the papers, she called Roland over to the table and had me explain to him. Although Roland had initially referred to Shirley as "her" because of the name he heard, he knew it was my dad after we spoke.

This Purple Paper was dated September 8, 2017, and it said, "Shirley started with a little pain in her back (lower). I never did much about it. In late December, my pain was much harder to handle. I did have cancer everywhere. All of the correct/right/perfect decisions were made." My dad had back pain for almost a year. He finally went to a hospital and was diagnosed with multiple myeloma, cancer of the bone marrow. He lived for four years but couldn't do a whole lot. After four years, the medication stopped working, and within a month he passed away.

The chances of getting one Purple Paper was certainly not a given, but to get two Purple Papers was really just incredible! It was what I so desperately needed. I had always believed in the afterlife and that our loved ones could communicate with us when they were gone, but my depression had gotten to such an all-time low that I just didn't know what I believed anymore. I truly felt like there was no life left for me. Although I have had suicidal thoughts for many years, I always believed that if someone commits suicide, they would have to immediately reincarnate and come back and live this life again and I just didn't want to do that! So I would pray to my dad to just take me, to do something so that I would die and be with him. Now that my mom was with him, I would pray to both of them to take me.

Since that day I found the strength and courage, because of those messages and because of the support of my dearest friends, to make a major life decision that was very difficult to do and came with many repercussions. I was moving to a new place and there were a lot of unknowns and I was terrified—me, who at one time in my life was so independent, was now scared of change. With the incredible losses over the last two years, and having already lost myself, I just didn't think there was a chance to have any kind of a productive life again. But here I am, on my own and actually believing that I will be able to build my life again. It's like everything collided all at once to save my soul—Roland, my angels, my mom, my dad, my friends—they all came together at just the right moment, and for that I am blessed and grateful.

Chapter 29

THE ROSARY BEADS

BY JOYCE MAIONE-PEZZULLI

I had tried for years to see Roland for a private reading but was never able to have one. When I finally had the opportunity to see him at one of his events, my expectations were as high as those of everyone else in the room. I was hoping Roland would share a message from someone in my family, especially my mother and brother. I was there with my daughter, Audra, and even though we thought we were early, the only two seats together were in the second row. I usually like to sit near the back so I won't be too conspicuous.

When Roland began explaining his method and other aspects of how he receives his messages (to be truthful, I really wasn't paying attention), I was only thinking, "OK, get on with the readings." He began to single out several people, behind me, to the sides of me, and in front of me, telling them what he heard, explaining who he saw standing with them. Halfway through his presentation, he took a break, and I was thinking there was still time for me to get a reading. My daughter got up to use the restroom, and while she was waiting, I saw Roland talking to her. I anxiously awaited her return to her seat, but Roland did not have much to say to her, just that there were a lot of spirits moving around her, but no message.

The second half continued much like the first half and I still didn't receive a message. At the end of the evening, Roland commented on how many people were waiting for a message and pointed to a couple of people. Then he pointed to me and asked who I wanted to hear from. I answered, "My father, my mother, and my brother Ralph." He asked how my brother had died. I said I did not know. My parents had found him in his bed after he had passed. Roland looked at me and then asked me to stay after to talk to him.

When my daughter and I approached Roland after the session, I was thrilled to learn that not only did he have a Purple Paper for me, but he had three of them, two of which were recorded before the event and one that he drew on while we were talking to him. On that one, he drew two stick people and the words "father and brother." He also stated that my brother died at 7:11 p.m.

I received my first Purple Paper; it was from my mother, Therese. I was not concerned with the spelling of my mother's name since I could relate to everything written on it, especially the drawing of rosary beads ("special beads") in the corner. She always had at least one pair of rosaries on her person at all times. She mentioned to Roland that I should "keep the beads," another confirmation that the message came from spirit for me. The paper read, "Theresa finally is peaceful. Tell my family that when I passed, I needed to find my mother. It was such a long time. I missed her so much. So when I say 'I'm fi-

Roland M. Comtois - The Purple Papers
Channeled Messages for the Soul
www.blessingsbyroland.com

11-6-2015

Theresa finally is peaceful. Tell my family that when I passed I needed to find my mother. It was so long time. I missed her so much. So when I say "I'm finally peaceful." is because I found her. Our lives were good. We were good. Heaven has been

nally peaceful,' [it] is because I found her. Our lives were good. We were good. Heaven has peace."

It stated that she had to find her mother, something she had worried about ever since her mother had passed. Her mother had been afraid to die, so when she did, my mother wanted assurance that my *mémère* was safe in heaven and at peace. I was so happy that they were together; my mother had missed her very much.

The second paper I received that evening was from my brother Ralph. It showed a person lying down inside a house with three hearts around him. My brother died in bed. He had three sons, whom he adored—Jeffrey, Matthew, and Nicholas. He had their names tattooed on his arm after each one was born and also had their names stenciled on his truck. Those hearts drawn on the paper unequivocally represented his love for his three sons. Also written on the paper was this: "I felt like I fell asleep, but it was an aneurysm. I felt a tingling feeling and passed away. I don't remember anything after 7:01. There was something about leaving the house. I didn't want to be late."

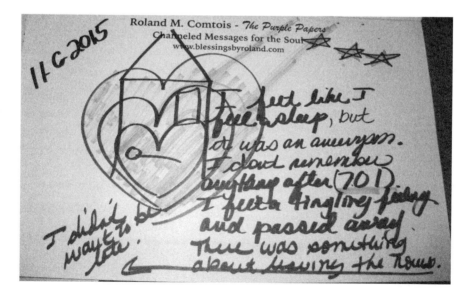

My brother had the same unbelievable old-world work ethic that my father had and was never late for work. I can't even remember a time when he called in sick; he was so dedicated to his job. He was even at work when he was having a heart attack two years prior to his passing, calling my parents to say only that he wasn't feeling well before they picked him up and brought him to the hospital. I met them at the hospital and was alone with my brother when he coded. Gratefully, the doctors brought him back to us. Of my four brothers, I was closest to Ralph, even more so because of that life-and-death experience. He would call me whenever he had a problem, which makes it strange that he never told me, or anyone, that he had an inoperable brain tumor. We knew he suffered from headaches, but we chalked it up to the stress of his job. We only found out about his tumor three months after he died and only because my mother went to the same doctor as Ralph, who told her his diagnosis.

Roland's Purple Paper said it was an aneurysm and that he went quickly. He had come home from work that day, had supper—his dishes were still in the sink, his keys and cell phone on the table—and took a shower. He must have had a bad headache because he apparently went straight from the shower to his bed. We believe he died on Saturday night, October 18, 2003, but he wasn't found until Monday, October 20, 2003, when his boss called my parents to tell them Ralph hadn't shown up for work. He was only forty-nine years old.

My mother died six months later, on April 15, 2004, on the morning she was to be discharged from the hospital. She had gone in for a colon operation and had progressed nicely. I went to see her every day and told her we would celebrate her birthday when she came home. The night before she died, the weather was really foggy. My mother worried about me driving at night, as I had only one good eye, and told me to stay home. "I'll see you tomorrow when I am discharged," she said. We argued about it, as mothers and their children tend to do, before I gave in to her wishes. She really did not want me to drive. I went home and took a short nap on the couch, waking up at 7:00 p.m., thinking that I would stop in for a quick visit before visiting hours were over at 8:00 p.m. but thought better of it. I would see her in the morning, I told myself.

The call came at midnight. The hospital said, "Tell your family to come to the hospital. Your mother is not doing well." I called my family, who all raced to the hospital. I was delayed trying to call one of my brothers, whom I hadn't yet reached. When I finally got in the car, I was further delayed by a driver with his emergency flashers on, going so slowly, and I couldn't pass him. My family made it to the hospital before me. I arrived there in time to hear my sister scream out in sadness as my mother passed away. I felt so guilty about not being there for her, for my family, for me. I do believe now that the delay was not happenstance. My mother passed the way she needed to go, without any unnatural intervention, and without me having to remember the painful reality of her final moments.

My father was diagnosed with prostate cancer not long after my mother passed. An active, hardworking man who was still on the job at eighty-five years of age, he died two years after my mother. He's with my brother Ralph Jr. and my mother now, along with my nana, his mother, each of them watching over the loved ones they left behind. How do I know that? When Roland gave me those messages from my mother, Therese Maione, and my brother, Ralph Maione Jr., the date on both of those Purple Papers was significant. They were both dated November 6, 2015, the same day my daughter was in a minor car accident. Somehow I don't think it was a coincidence. I believe they were both there, watching over my daughter from heaven, making sure she was safe, and they wanted me know that.

Chapter 30

DAD

ANONYMOUS

I lost my dad on December 12, 2015. My husband knew I was having a hard time with my father's passing, so he wanted to get me tickets to see Roland. It was funny because the first time he looked on Roland's website to see where Roland might be hosting an event, he couldn't find any events near us. Then he looked again a little while later, and suddenly a show opened in Rhode Island. I didn't know it at the time, but that was the first sign that my father was still here.

When we arrived at the event, I was skeptical. I wasn't sure what to expect if anything at all. It was a small, intimate crowd, and Roland came into the room with a binder full of Purple Papers. He started talking to all of us about what he did and heard, and then proceeded to talk to certain people about their loved ones. His presentation was almost halfway over, and he hadn't said anything to us. Then, he took me by surprise as he walked over to me and said, "You don't think your dad would talk in front of everybody, do you?" It caught me off guard, and I really didn't know what to do. He was right. My father was a very quiet man and wouldn't have wanted to speak about personal subjects in front of others.

After his break, Roland came back to me and started saying things to both my husband and me that he would not have any way of knowing. He was saying that I comforted my dad while he was in the hospital. While Roland was speaking, he kept stroking his right arm, which is what I had done to my dad in the hospital. He told me that I was my dad's favorite and that he loved my husband like a son.

Then he asked me what my dad's name was and when he had passed and handed me a folded Purple Paper. I didn't read it until we got into the car. Then I just sat there numb. What was written on the paper dated May 15, 2016, along with my father's name, were words that indicated exactly how he felt and how he would speak: "Joseph didn't want to tell you how bad it really was for him. A couple of months before I passed, I was so sick. My stomach—back—pressure. I had enough of this stuff. I'm OK now."

My father was a diabetic and had his leg amputated, which put him in a wheelchair. He had just come home from rehab after recuperating from a mild stroke and relearning how to get himself from his bed to his wheelchair when he became ill again and had to return to the hospital. This was in October 2015. I was very close with my dad and could tell from hearing his voice on the phone that he had given up. He couldn't really talk clearly because the stroke had affected his speech, but he always used to joke with me and he wasn't joking anymore.

He was finally able to go back home in the beginning of December, only to be readmitted to the hospital. My father lived in Mississippi, so we flew out as soon as we could. When I arrived at the hospital to see him, he was coherent enough to know I was there. He recognized me, but less than an hour later, he started to decline. When I got there, I held his right hand and kept rubbing his arm. That was why when Roland said that I was stroking my dad's right arm and that my dad said this was comforting to him, it really freaked me out. There is no way he would know that. My dad was in a lot of pain in the hospital, and he could only communicate that to me by squeezing my hand whenever I asked if he was hurting. That's another reason why the Purple Paper meant everything to me. I knew he was in a lot of pain in the hospital, but he never told me before that. It just all made sense to me after receiving that message from Roland. I have no doubt my dad communicated to Roland. When Roland said, "You were his favorite," I believe that to be true too. He also used to tell my husband that he always felt he was part of the family and he loved him like his son. He reconfirmed that through Roland.

It's strange to say but I never felt more at peace after that session with Roland. I know that was my dad speaking to us. I read my Purple Paper when I need some reassurance. That session helped me to understand that my dad may have passed, but his spirit will always be with me.

Chapter 31

TOUCHED BY AN ANGEL

ANONYMOUS

The young mother of two sons, ages three and five, I was pregnant with my third child when I found out that my baby girl would be born with Down syndrome. The thought of raising a child with disabilities seemed challenging at the least. This was especially so when I unexpectedly found myself to be a single mother shortly after she was born.

My daughter was a joy the minute she was born, bringing with her an infectious smile and love of life that has since enchanted everyone she meets. Her brothers doted on her, and I couldn't imagine not having her in our lives.

As it turned out, I wasn't alone in that feeling.

Steve had been a family friend for years and had never married. He was a happy guy, very smart and so funny, living a life of fun and fancy, unencumbered by challenges of raising children. But he was also one of the most caring men I have ever met, stepping into our lives just when we desperately needed it.

I remember reminding him that I was the single mother of three little ones when he asked me to marry him, incredulous that he had even considered it. That did not deter him. In fact, I think it made him even more convinced that I, we, were the perfect family for him.

He valued life to the nth degree, loving all living beings to the fullest, especially a precious little girl with special needs who was smitten with him from the minute they met. Steve's love of life was heightened when he was revived after a motorcycle accident a few years before we were married. He was pronounced dead but was saved by a doctor who happened upon the scene at just the right time. So grateful to have been given a second chance at life, he would gather friends and family together every year on the anniversary of his accident to celebrate his rebirth!

After we were married, our family became a true presence in our town. People would comment on seeing Steve at church, with our little girl's arms wrapped around him, and at the ball games, scouting, and PTO events. Everyone knew this wonderful family man and our three bright, sociable children—and everyone loved Princess Kate, as he fondly called our little daughter.

But one day, after nine amazing and happy years of marriage, I received a call from the police while I was in a meeting at my daughter's school. "There's been an accident," I heard the person on the other end of the phone say. "Your husband didn't make it." I didn't believe what I heard and knew I had to get to the hospital to be by his side. A teacher at the school was kind enough to drive me there. When I saw Steve lying there lifeless in the emergency room and heard the words "blunt force trauma" as the cause of his death, I collapsed in anguish. That sounded horrible. Had he suffered? Was he alone? Was there much pain? I sat with him for a long time trying to make sense of this life-changing moment. I had kissed him goodbye just hours before. How was it possible that he was gone?

I was told that another driver hit his motorcycle head-on. It was an accident, they told me, and Steve didn't have a chance. Steve loved motorcycles and had purchased a red Ducati just a couple of weeks before. He couldn't wait to take his Italian-made motorbike on the road. Stylish, sophisticated, and a technological dream, Ducatis are among the most sought-after motorcycles by enthusiasts who are seduced by their beauty and handling. This was his dream bike, and, as I learned after his passing, it was also the second one he had purchased. He had been riding on his first red Ducati, the same model as the one he had just recently purchased, when he had his first "fatal" accident. This time, though, there was no doctor on the scene to bring him back to life.

My friend tried to get me to see Roland for a long time. I finally agreed to accompany her to a radio studio in Rhode Island where Roland was doing a live show. I wasn't sure what I was doing there, so I was a little nervous and didn't speak a word. Roland seemed to keep looking at me all during the show and shuffling through a big stack of Purple Papers. It unnerved me at the time, and I felt uncomfortable. Finally, at the end of the show, he called me up to the table where he was sitting with his stacks of papers. "I have a message for you," he said, and he gave me a Purple Paper.

Roland knew all about my husband's passing without any of us saying a word. It was a motorcycle accident, he told me. He said that Steve died immediately at the accident scene. He felt no pain. The angels were with him. He wasn't alone.

"I just slid off to the side," read the words on the paper. "I passed away at the scene. I couldn't get my bike under control. I didn't have any time to get control." Roland assured me that he did not suffer and no one was to blame. Those were the two questions that kept going through my mind, causing the endless sleepless nights and anguish during my waking hours! He also told me that Steve loves me very much. That is something that every wife never gets tired of hearing and longs to hear once her spouse is no longer with us.

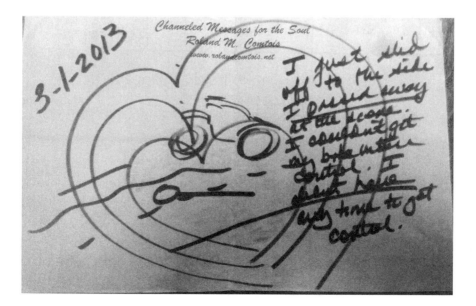

I had been getting signs from my husband before that night. Pictures in my house mysteriously moved and one even dropped to the floor to get my attention. One was a photograph of my husband and our daughter; in it they were both smiling as they shared a special moment together. While I was comforted by the fact that Steve was still with us in spirit, the Purple Paper message from Roland confirmed for me that he was OK, that he passed quickly in the arms of his fellow angels. I no longer held the anger that had consumed me when I learned he was hit by another car. I let go of that as I finally forgave the driver.

I learned the meaning of unconditional everlasting love from my husband. And I also learned how to forgive. Those two priceless gifts are a part of Steve's legacy. But there's so much more as well. I learned that angels really do exist, and while they may not be able to stay on earth forever, they are here for a reason. Steve was brought back from his first "death" to bring life to my children and me after we were abandoned all those years ago. I do believe that he was an angel with a job to do. And while he could only be with us for nine short but fulfilling years, the memories, kindness, and love he showed and shared will stay with us forever.

Chapter 32

MY SISTER KELLY

BY VERONICA (MULLALY) PEARSON

My sister Kelly was everything to me. Seven years older and wise beyond her years, she was my best friend, my confidante, my mentor, my rock, my second mom. I was a latchkey kid growing up, so Kelly stepped in to fill my mother's shoes when she was at work. She cooked for me, helped me with my homework, listened to my complaints, dried my tears, told me stories, and shared many a laugh with me. Smart, funny, sometimes snarky, and always selfless, she would go above and beyond to make people happy. She lived, I think, to put a smile on everyone's face. I know she did on mine and my kids' too. She moved into our in-law apartment when my daughter Zoey was just three months old, with my son Steven being born two years later. She was a preschool teacher and a natural with kids. She didn't have any children of her own so mine became hers and she loved them unconditionally. My children loved their auntie dearly.

She became sick four years after she moved in with us. It was shortly after Mother's Day in 2014 when she was diagnosed with gallbladder cancer. She didn't tell us how bad it was as she put up the good fight, even during the worst of the bad days. As she began to slow down, I upped my game, taking care of her like she did for me all those years when we were growing up. I became her everything as our roles reversed. I cooked, cleaned, shopped, brought her to and from the doctors, and later took her to the hospital. During the last ten months we were together, the cancer had spread to her lungs and throughout her bones, causing unspeakable pain that she kept to herself.

She lost her fight in March 2016, a few days after suffering a massive stroke. Her doctors told us there was nothing more we could do. I lost a huge part of me that day and couldn't imagine life without her. But I also worried that I hadn't done enough for her, that maybe there was something I should have, could have, done for her that I neglected to do. My heart was very heavy with worry and sadness.

Then one day I happened to be watching Roland's live Facebook show, in which he talked about his Purple Papers and shared messages that were waiting to be delivered.

There was a message for me that day from her. Roland actually said my name as he delivered my sister's words: "Veronica, I have a message for you from your sister." That really caught my attention! Her message was channeled over the airways and the internet and down from the heavens right to me, and then again on a Purple Paper message that lifted the immense weight I was carrying and allowed me to breathe again.

Dated April 17, 2016, the Purple Paper reads, "Kelly wants you to know that the struggle is finally over. Even though, because of my age, I passed young, I had a good life. Tell Mom. I'm with her all the time. Hey Sis!!!!! Hey Mom!!! You should see me now!" The drawings on the paper were equally telling as they included a sketch of the doctor's office, the hospital, and home. There were three hearts embracing the home, indicating the love we all share.

My sister still checks on me, visiting in my dreams and in sudden temperature changes that alert me to her presence. Thanks to the Purple Paper message, I know she's OK now, and she knows that I am too.

Chapter 33

I AM FREE

BY MONIKA

I lost my son less than three months before attending Roland's Validating the Afterlife presentation. I desperately hoped for a message, a sign that would let me know he was finally at peace. I watched as Roland held up his trademark Purple Papers and said that so many loved ones lost had made their way here to give their people a message. Some were claimed on the spot; others were waiting to be claimed. During one of Roland's brief breaks, I found myself going up to the table to ask about a Purple Paper that I thought could be from my son. After reading it, nothing resonated with me. I didn't recognize anything on the paper that indicated it was from my son.

I turned to leave but turned back as Roland's assistant was flipping through the papers to find one for someone else. As she was doing so, a word jumped out at me, grabbing my attention and my heart: "heroin." I asked her for a closer look and in reading the rest of the Purple Paper, I knew, without a shadow of a doubt, that my son had sent me a message. Everything on the paper pointed to being from my son—his love of our home, once his grandparents' house, and his battle with addiction. At the bottom of the paper were the words, "I am free."

It read, "No more heroin…No more guilt…No more pain. I love you, Mom. I love how you never gave up. I never lost my way as badly as I did in the last few years. I am free."

Roland looked at me and told me that my son was standing there, and at that moment I felt his presence. I felt some peace.

At the end of the evening, Roland held my Purple Paper up to the audience and read it aloud to everyone in the room. As he spoke, you could feel the energy from others helping me through it. I was enveloped with a feeling of comfort and love that was truly palpable. It was beyond amazing—and healing.

Then the unimaginable happened. Roland held up another Purple Paper and said that one was from my son David too. And again, it was him, everything was him. The paper read, "For the first time, Mom, I can say I'm free—no more drugs—tell Dad too. He'll be so proud of me. I needed to leave the house. And I really needed to come back. I'm sorry for what I put you through. Yes, you are strong."

3-28.2017 Roland M. Comtois - *The Purple Papers*
Channeled Messages for the Soul
www.blessingsbyroland.com

For the first time, mom, I can really say I'm free — No more drugs — Tell Dad too. He'll be so proud of me. I needed to leave the house. And, I really needed to come back. I'm sorry for what I put you through. Yes, You are strong.

Another, dated January 12, 2018, read, "David isn't afraid of anything now. You've got to tell Dad how much I love him too. 'Let's go for a ride in my nice old car.' I fought really hard during some years of my life. I really want you to know how 'easy' my soul is. I love you guys."

1-12-2018 Roland M. Comtois - *The Purple Papers*
www.RolandComtois.net

David isn't afraid of anything now.
You've got to tell Dad how much I
love him too. "Let's go for a ride in
my new old car. I fought really hard
turning love parts of my life. I really
want you to know how "easy" my
soul is. I love you guys.

My son believed in the afterlife and knew I believed in it too. Even through my darkest days after his passing, I knew he would reach out to let me know he was happy, safe, and free.

Chapter 34

GRATEFUL TEARS

BY DEANNA J. HARMON

In September 2016, a dear friend of mine whom I met online posted on my Facebook timeline a live feed of Roland sharing messages. She sent me a message saying, "Dee, I think Roland has messages for you from heaven, from your son." And so it all began.

As I listened to Roland, he came to two Purple Papers that were unquestionably from my son Wayne, who had taken his own life two years earlier. Roland had his name specifically and on those two Purple Papers were messages that portrayed exactly what my son was like. His personality has not changed in spirit. My son had come to Roland in spirit on two different occasions, July 27, 2015, and September 13, 2016. As I was listening to this in the privacy of my home, my tears started to flow. I knew the messages were my son by the huge flow of love and the indescribable "knowing" that enveloped me, heart, body, mind, and soul. There was no doubt that these messages came from my beautiful "empath" son.

Simply defined, empaths are highly sensitive people who seem to feel other people's emotions. They are described as very kind, big-hearted people, generous to a fault and born nurturers. They tend to take on others' pain as they try to help those who are suffering. They are also known to love animals and nature.

Their kindness and empathy toward others takes a toll, often leaving the empath emotionally and physically drained and often depressed. Sometimes it feels like they are too fragile for life because they are often upset with things they see and read. I have learned that empaths have a rare gift in that they are uniquely selfless and always want to give of themselves. Knowing one, like my son Wayne, is more precious still.

His first message, written in July by Roland, was as follows: "Wayne wants you not to be worried about him. I asked for help 'on the other side' when I got there. You were so good to me—all the time! P.S. I wish I would've made it easier on you."

Roland M. Comtois - *The Purple Papers*
Channeled Messages for the Soul
www.blessingsbyroland.com

7-27-2015

Wayne wants you not to be worried about him. I asked for help 'on the other side' when I got there. You were so good to me — all the time!

My son came to Roland again on September 13, 2016. He is very persistent, as he always was here on earth. "Mom, I never made it out of the house. I know you wonder what happened or what went wrong." My son never made it out of our pole barn (through him, Roland described a building that is in fact our pole barn, not our house, but we had a living space there). "Everything got fuzzy. My head felt funny. You know I was having troubles—I want you to know that I will always be grateful for how hard you tried." I knew he was having troubles, but I didn't know he struggled so deeply to the point of crossing himself. "I love you, Mom" he said.

9-13-2016 Roland M. Comtois - *The Purple Papers*
Channeled Messages for the Soul
www.blessingsbyroland.com

Mom, I never made it out of the house. I know you wonder what happened or what went wrong. Everything got fuzzy. My head felt funny. You know I was having troubles—I want you to know that I will always be grateful for how hard you tried. I love you mom.

When I received the messages through Roland, I burst into grateful tears. I knew without a doubt it was my son wanting to get through to me, to let me know he is well. The messages confirm what I had felt in my heart. My son came to me one day after he transitioned; at that time I thought I was losing it. Roland's messages brought much comfort, healing, and peace for me.

I gave birth to my son in 1994. I was a very young mother, and from birth there was something about the immediate bond we shared that resonated with me, like two old souls meeting again. He was not only my son, but he was my best friend for twenty years. I had him at age nineteen. Looking back, he was always very sensitive, kind, loving, and giving. He graduated from high school in 2012. I think he was struggling to find his way after that. He loved nature, his dog, Sadie, our cats—any and all animals. He also loved sitting in our woods watching wildlife. He taught himself how to play guitar. He was artistic and enjoyed drawing, but his biggest passion was family, especially me, his little sister, and my husband. He was so funny, always making jokes and making others laugh, pulling little pranks. His humor was endless, and so were his compliments to others, especially regarding my cooking. When I spoke to Roland on the telephone, he mentioned my son's humor, and I confirmed with Roland that, in fact, that was one of his biggest traits I miss the most.

On September 16, 2014, I went into our pole barn. My son was in there listening to music. We talked for a little while before I told him good night and that I loved him. He said, "I love you too, Mom." I closed the door, went to bed, and woke the next morning to every mother's worst nightmare. I found my son hanging in our pole barn. He had transitioned himself in the early morning hours of September 17, 2014, sometime between 4:30 and 5:00 a.m. He was just twenty years old.

The biggest thing I wish for all to know is that because someone struggles with depression and they transition by suicide, it's about the heart. Suicide does not define my son—it's not who he is. There are not always signs that someone is struggling. My son had just purchased a car two months prior. I did not sense anything wrong when I was out with him the night before. He didn't leave a note.

So be kind. Be loving like my son was and still is. You never truly know what someone may be struggling with. Roland's messages comforted me in so many ways. My son in spirit knew I had concerns about how he transitioned. I feel that is why he contacted Roland and gave me a blessing of peace, healing, and comfort that love never dies.

I have always known there is more to life than what we experience here, and Wayne confirmed it through Roland. He is now healed and in pure love. When a loved one transitions, you can still talk to them. They hear you, and the bond is unbreakable. My son has come to me in divine ways like through Roland's channeled messages. But I receive many other signs as well. He sends me dragonflies and coins. I get them through my son's guitar picks, music on the radio, and orbs in photos I take. Our fur babies also know and react when my son is present.

Let's do grief in a whole new light. It's OK to cry, it's OK to scream, it's OK to not be OK. It's OK to believe. The power of eternal love can make hearts whole again, and that's more than OK with me.

In memory of Wayne Daniel (January 19, 1994–September 17, 2014).

Chapter 35

THROUGH THE DISTANCE
BY JANINE JACKSON

I received my Purple Paper right before Thanksgiving 2013. The first thing I remember is the date on the paper because it was the day a friend had contacted me because he thought I needed to go see Roland.

To make a kind of long story short, my father was diagnosed with multiple myeloma on July 3, 2007. When I left for a business trip to Atlanta a week later, he was in great spirits and looking forward to summer.

Three days into my trip, he was admitted to the hospital with pneumococcal pneumonia and placed on a ventilator and into a medically induced coma so his lungs could recover. I rushed to get home but never again saw him conscious. For the next few weeks, his lungs, given a respite from working on their own, continued to recover. By July 29, he was breathing 95 percent on his own and was scheduled to come off the ventilator the next day. Unfortunately, sometime during the night, he had a massive nonrecoverable stroke. We made the gut-wrenching decision to remove him from life support.

The night I saw Roland, he gave me a message from my father. He said that he wanted me to know that he knows I did everything possible to get home, which gave me some closure about being away on the business trip. I also knew my father, a man who was the life of any party, would not have wanted to live with effects of a stroke or the restrictions of the disease he had been diagnosed with. My nephew had that disease as well and had to avoid being near crowds or children. A people person who loved everyone of every age, my father wouldn't have been able to live like that. The paper confirmed that he would not have recovered from the stroke, that he had had enough. That Purple Paper gave me such peace.

It read, "Let's face it; I never recovered from the stroke. I didn't/couldn't recover (no matter how hard we tried). I did walk peacefully to heaven. You know, I just had enough of this. I love you."

Roland also mentioned that my father was with his brothers (he had four), and they had made peace with their father. My grandfather died when Dad was a preteen. Because he had passed so long ago, before I was even born, I was unaware of the estrangement between my grandfather and his sons. An older cousin since confirmed this for me.

I will admit I was a bit of a skeptic before seeing Roland, but that night made me a believer.

Chapter 36

MY FOREVER TRUE LOVE

BY SANDRA RUSSELL

My husband, James, and I were only married for five years, but during our time together, I realized what true love really was. He was much older than me, and we married later in life. I like to believe that the universe saved the best for last for both of us.

We lived happily with the cats and kittens we took in during that time, along with a dog we both were attached to. Ours was a happy home and we felt blessed to have found each other. James was a good and kind man who always tried to do the right thing. He was a lifelong smoker and wanted to quit before it affected his health and our lives together. But try as he might, with patches, nicotine gum, and all the other remedies available for people who wanted to stop smoking, he could not break his habit.

He developed breathing problems before the doctors told him he had lung cancer. By the time we found out, the cancer had gone into his brain. It seemed to happen so quickly. In just six weeks, James went from feeling on top of the world to passing away from cancer.

It all started one late December evening when he was having trouble breathing and wasn't feeling well. He went straight to bed before dinner. I checked on him often and helped him get off the bed so he could go into the bathroom. He didn't have the strength to walk on his own. He kept telling me that he was sorry, so very sorry, and then started making nonsensical statements. I made light of his comments and put him back to bed.

In the morning, he still wasn't feeling well and hadn't eaten, so I brought him some soup. He was not able to keep it or any other liquid down. His conversation, what little of it he could manage by then, became more disjointed as the days wore on, and I knew something was terribly wrong. I did the best I could to help him and make him comfortable, but it soon became too much for both of us. His breathing had gotten much worse and his mind was not the same.

We got him admitted to a hospital in Boston where his prognosis was grim. He was only there for a few weeks before he passed away on January 22, 1995.

I lost my brother and mother in the years that followed, along with the pets my husband and I had loved. I felt their loss every day.

It wasn't until May 2016 that I had the opportunity to attend one of Roland's events at the Stadium Theatre in Woonsocket, Rhode Island. Although our families were close, I had not realized that Roland had the gift of spiritual communication. I was not sure what to expect at his presentation, but I was interested in seeing what he did. To my surprise, in an auditorium that held hundreds of people, he gave me two Purple Papers that night. They were

8-4-2016 Roland M. Comtois - *The Purple Papers*
Channeled Messages for the Soul
www.blessingsbyroland.com

Please tell my wife that she did her best "you're right." I went through so much. I wish we could've had a longer married life." JAMES.
P.S. I love "all" the kittens and cats over the years.
I love you.

from my husband, James. They were filled with words of love that I will always cherish.

Roland shared that James was talking about his breathing problems. The first Purple Paper said, "Please tell my wife that she did her best. You're right I went through so much. I wish we could have had a longer married life." Roland also wrote, "P.S. I loved all the kittens and cats over the years. I love you."

The other said, "James fought a breathing battle. 6–7 weeks before I passed, I was overwhelmed with everything. I didn't want to 'linger' or 'wait.' I had to go home because it was too much for me."

I still miss him dearly and love him so much. He fought so hard for everything. I take great comfort in knowing that he has found peace now and no longer needs to struggle.

Chapter 37

PENNIES FROM HEAVEN
BY JENNY HALLORAN

My friend Diane invited me and three close friends to join her for a healing circle and evening of meditation with Roland Comtois in December of 2011. Diane thought we could all benefit from Roland's healing and channeling abilities. Roland was, after all, an internationally renowned medium with a reputation for spiritual healing who had touched many lives immeasurably. There were thirty-three others there as well, strangers who at night's end would feel a connection to one another that transcended expectations. I didn't know what to expect, but I came away with a gift from my friend Diane (who brought me to the event as a present) that could never be repaid. I could spend a long time describing the evening and what took place with the other friends I made that night, but I will stick to my story, my experience, and the priceless evening with my deceased brother, Jeff.

Roland singled me out of the group the minute we sat down. He told me I was surrounded by a lot of white light, which meant there was a lot of love around me. He asked me why I was there. I told him I really didn't know; my friend had taken me and I was open to anything. He smiled and moved on.

A little bit later in the evening, he asked me how I was doing. I told him I was fine, but he didn't seem to believe me. He kept looking at me and asking me why I came. He asked me why I spent all this money to attend this event. I told him my friend took me as a gift, and I had not paid anything. He continued to stare at me trying to figure out what I wanted. He repeatedly asked me if I was OK, and I repeatedly said I was fine.

Now let me clarify that when Roland welcomed us that evening, he made it a point to tell everyone he was doing a healing meditation, not a channeling session. If he got any messages, he said, he would pass them along. But he made it clear that he was not there to communicate with those who have passed on. So needless to say, I was not about to ask him if he could get a message from Jeff for me.

But he kept coming back to me, at least four or five times, to ask if I were OK, and what I had hoped to receive that night. I finally said I was hoping to hear from my brother. Roland looked relieved to finally be able to understand why I was there. As soon as I told him what I had hoped for, Jeff came through. The only thing Roland asked me was my brother's name, and once I gave it to him, the communication opened up.

The first thing Roland felt was a feeling of someone being lost and struggling before his passing. After a few moments, he waved his hands and bounced on his toes and kind of mockingly said, "Look at me, I'm in heaven. I made it. I'm in heaven." He then wanted me to know he was "not broken," and with this, Roland seemed perplexed as to how Jeff had passed away. Once I told him that his lower arm had been amputated in order to save his life from a lethal infection, it seemed to make sense. He then communicated, "I know there was no time" and "I know there was no time to say goodbye." He seemed to imply that the hardest thing for him was being unable to communicate. Roland put his hand to his neck and said the words were right here, but Jeff couldn't get them out, "I could not tell anyone how I felt."

"You had a terrible decision to make, but you made the right decision, so thank you." We did have to make a gut-wrenching decision to stop taking more extreme measures to save his life because all quality of life would have been lost. One can only imagine the weight taken off our shoulders by him saying the words "right decision" and "thank you."

He then said, "Finish what you started."

My brother, through Roland, then proceeded to tell me he leaves funny signs, but I never see them. He implies he leaves me pennies, but I never believe they are from him. After Jeff died, I told my children that whenever they see a penny, pick it up; it means someone is thinking of you. So this reference made a lot of sense to me.

He was right too when he said I believed I never got any signs from him. My sister got signs, but I never did. Roland said that Jeff wanted me to know that "I leave you signs all the time, but you never believe them. I try so hard to send you signs. I want you to find peace." I had to admit that ever since Jeff had passed, I asked and wondered why he never left me signs.

"My sister needs to know that I'm the one who sends her signs, right? I sat with you last night while you stared at my picture. I REALLY, REALLY love you," he wrote through Roland on a cherished Purple Paper dated February 12, 2012.

Roland's comments gave me pause. I started to think about the pennies. For some time after Jeff's passing, I would pick up the pennies I found. I would check the date to see if it would be a reference to Jeff, and after a while, I told myself this was foolish. When we went to visit my mom in November 2011 for her eightieth birthday (Jeff had passed in 2005), I found a penny on my nightstand in the hotel room. For a brief moment I thought about checking the date. Then I admonished myself for even thinking about it, so I never looked at it.

When I got back from Roland's event that evening of the meditation, I told my husband, Jim, about the pennies and how Jeff had said that he left me pennies. Jim proceeded to go to our bedroom and take out a penny that was stuck in our doorframe for years! I never saw it and didn't know it was there. To put some of this in perspective, I had visited my mother on Tuesday, November 29. I went to Roland's event a few days later on Friday, December 2. On Sunday the fourth, I went up to bed, physically and emotionally drained from my weekend and my evening with Roland. Sitting next to my tweezers on my window ledge was a penny. The date on it was 1982, the year I graduated. I said to myself that it had to be from Jeff.

I then realized what I had purchased in Florida earlier in the week, before my evening with Roland. When we were at the Edison and Ford Winter Estates, I purchased one thing in the gift store to bring home. It was a giant penny! I have no idea why I picked up this penny to buy. I remember thinking it would be great to put it in my son's Christmas stocking, but really why I picked that out from all the Edison and Ford memorabilia was beyond me—until that evening. It all made sense.

And then I realized something else. My kids, all four of them, watch the movie *Elf* all the time. Even though it is a Christmas movie, they watch it year-round. They watched it in the car all fall. My son Connor and his girlfriend watched it over Thanksgiving. One of the songs from that movie is "Pennies from Heaven." There are no coincidences. I have been left other pennies. Deliberately placed pennies, all in very odd places.

According to Roland, Jeff seemed frustrated I wasn't finding the pennies he was leaving, so he said he would leave "five pennies next time." I was hoping to come across a row or pile of pennies somewhere plain as day. I was in New York City the day after Roland's event and thought for sure I would find my pennies. Instead, I found myself standing in front of a statue of Gertrude Stein in Bryant Park. All I remember from packing up Jeff's apartment were all the Gertrude Stein books I packed up, and, embarrassingly, I didn't know who she was. Now, here I was Christmas shopping in New York City with the girls from work, and I stopped to look down for pennies and saw I was at the foot of a statue, a statue of Gertrude Stein. Coincidence?

On Christmas Eve I was unpacking a bag of wrapped gifts to bring downstairs now that the kids were asleep. As I took off the top layer of presents, there sat a nickel (five cents, my five pennies) directly placed, dead center in the middle of a package. Now the funny thing about this package was it was for the dogs, and though the paper didn't cover the end of the package completely, leaving about a square inch not covered in wrapping paper, I didn't think it mattered—it was for the dogs. There sitting in that square unwrapped inch was the nickel, perfectly centered. Now, if Jeff were going to make an appearance, Christmas Eve would be the night. He always spent it with us.

Later in December of that year, I had dinner with my best friend Christy for our monthly girl's night out. We were talking about Jeff and Roland and as our dinner was coming out, I ran into the bathroom. There in the middle of the rug was a shiny penny. When we stepped up to buy our movie tickets an hour later, another shiny penny glowed up at me from the middle of the welcome mat. I believe these were left by Jeff. Jeff knew Christy well since we had been friends since we were both four.

Through Roland, Jeff reassured me he is at all of my daughter's performances. You see, Jeff and my daughter Hannah shared a love for musical theater. He said it was obvious he was there, and he mentioned sitting in seat 11. He told me to pay attention. It would be obvious he was there. That spring Hannah was cast in *Around the World in Eighty Days*. There were twenty-five actors, she was actor number eleven, in seat 11. The following year she was cast as Penny Sycamore in *You Can't Take It with You*. The irony doesn't escape any of us. Hannah said there was always a penny to be found on stage, and my other daughter Kelly often finds them as well.

Summer of 2012 found me in Brazil at a spiritual retreat for two weeks. The first person I met was a woman who told me she had recently lost her brother. After a brief conversation on the staircase, she told me, "It was nice meeting you, Penny. I will see you at dinner." I felt remiss in reminding her my name was Jenny, so I didn't. The owner of the posada and spiritual guide would yell out as she drove pass me walking down the street, "Penny, darling, would you like a ride?" When I purchased a bottle of water, she asked, "Now what room are you staying in, Penny?" I think Jeff was enjoying playing this game with me. He had told Roland he would send me funny signs and sounds—he had everyone calling me Penny.

During the evening with Roland, Jeff thanked my friend Diane for bring-ing me. Roland said he felt Jeff had a sarcastic personality. He said he felt a wit about him. "I know she's a lot of work," Jeff said to Diane through Roland, referring to me. "Well, maybe just a little bit of work." He thanked Diane for being there for me.

He went on to tell me, "You are a better writer than you think; finish what *you* started. You aren't as good as me, but you are not bad. Finish what you started." Now the only thing this could mean is a poem I wrote the year he died called "Our Santa," and true, I never finished it. It is the only thing I have written since he died that wasn't for work or a card to someone.

Roland said he got the feeling Jeff was going to a gig. He kind of snapped his fingers and said, "I feel he is going to a gig and needs to get going." His friends always said heaven was probably being blessed with a new musical. You see, Jeff was a lyricist and writer. He then said again to finish what I started and laughed. "Good luck. Finish what you started." And he was gone.

Since that first evening with Roland, other members of my family have received messages from Jeff. He reached out to my husband to assure him that his brother Frank, who passed suddenly on July 5, 2015, was OK. The Purple Paper, dated just six weeks after Frank's death, said, "Jimmy…I got him…Don't worry."

On subsequent Purple Papers, Jeff reminded me that he knows I "hear the music," and he asks teasingly, "Can you still see me playing the piano? I am so glad you taught me everything I know (except the piano)." One of his best-known songs he had written was "Music Is Healing"; the synchronicity doesn't escape me. And yes, I do hear the music. When visiting a sacred wa-terfall in Brazil, in the utter silence, I asked my friend, "Do you hear the mu-sic?" She said she did not. On a visit to Florida one summer, as my mother, the kids, and I were crossing the town green, an orchestra playing in the ga-zebo all of a sudden started "Pennies from Heaven." My daughter looked at me and smiled. Yes, I hear the music, Jeff.

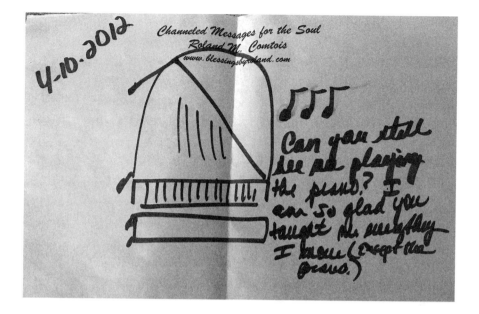

My mother passed suddenly on April 26, 2016. Her favorite flowers were daisies. That's what I always sent her, and daisies were the only flowers at her small service. A few weeks before she died, I had purchased tickets for another one of Roland's events and had planned to bring a friend with me. I never imagined that my mother would be gone then, or that I would get a message from her at the event.

But there it was. It was dated May 17, 2016, and it read, "It's important that my daughter knows that I saw such a light and beautiful peace surrounded me. Yes, around me … I will leave one flower … I love you so much." In the middle of the Purple Paper, there was the prettiest daisy you ever saw.

Roland M. Comtois - *The Purple Papers*
Channeled Messages for the Soul
www.blessingsbyroland.com

5-17-2016

It's important that my daughter knows that I . . . saw such a light and beautiful peace surrounded around me . . . Yes—I will leave our flower . . . . I love you so much.

Like Jeff, Mom has found her way to heaven and has also found a voice through Roland. The gift of eternal love just keeps on giving!

I still am not exactly sure why Jeff said, "Finish what you started." Was it the poem, was it my own spiritual journey, or was it an awakening to so much more? Jeff also said more than once in communication with Roland, "Tell my story." So Jeff, I am, I am telling your story through this book. I hope it brings peace to others knowing that love is eternal, love surpasses space and time. Signs can be found in a public bathroom, a windowsill, across the world in another country, and, if you are really lucky, in a Purple Paper.

And yes, music is healing, words are healing, signs are healing. If we stay open to it all, healing begins. We are all here to use our gifts, whatever form they take to transform lives through love and light. I am so very grateful Roland shared his gift with me that evening. I have learned to see the signs and stop and pause when I do, connecting with spirit and the love that surrounds it.

One of my Purple Papers said, "I know you hear the music. I try so hard to send you signs. I want you to find peace."

Jeff, I have found peace.

Chapter 38

THE PROMISE OF PEACE
BY NICOLE M. LEBLANC

My cousin Jay, Jason Paul Mendes, was like a brother to me. I grew up in a large family, with twenty-six cousins. When I was a kid, my mom and my aunt were very close, so our families would spend many summers together at our cottage, finding periwinkles, walking the beach, building forts, and just having fun. Jay and I shared so many great times together. He was a happy, energetic all-star quarterback who loved—and was loved by—everyone.

It was a sad day when he, always healthy and vibrant, was diagnosed with a glioblastoma, a tumor caused by a very aggressive and common malignant brain cancer for which there is no cure. It was in an area that could not be operated on due to the proximity of the tumor in relation to the spine. As my life path had led me to learning about natural healing and becoming a Reiki Master, I was determined to help Jay overcome and beat this. I researched tirelessly. I read about various healing modalities from Edgar Cayce, sent Jay crystals used to balance the energy systems, contacted holistic healers, sent distant Reiki healing and prayed really hard. God had other plans when he took Jay from our family on March 18, 2011. He passed into his eternal resting place at only thirty-three years old, leaving behind a family, a wife, and two beautiful young daughters.

After that, I struggled with my belief in natural healing and energy healing because they didn't work for Jay, and I questioned everything. I knew that becoming a Reiki Master was all about supporting others with healing energy, but I had a more personal agenda in mind when I studied Reiki. I not only wanted to send healing energy to Jay, I wanted to cure him. This often is a conflict that many healers are confronted with; they are not supposed to put their ego and needs ahead of what is best for their clients. This turned out to be an important lesson on my own journey. I remember giving Jay Reiki shortly before he passed and sending him peaceful relaxing thoughts to make an easy transition. Believing in spirit and the afterlife was reassuring to me as I envisioned him going to a much better place. But I couldn't be absolutely sure that such a place existed until I received some sort of sign that he was OK and no longer in pain.

I finally received the confirmation I needed from Roland when he gave me a Purple Paper at a presentation at the Unity Radiant Light in Providence, Rhode Island. I had no expectations of receiving a message. As a fellow Reiki practitioner, I just wanted to be in his energy.

I remember Roland coming up to me, looking me in the eye, placing his hands on his head, and asking me, "Whose head hurt? Who did you try to save?" Jay came to mind right away, as it had been just about six months since he had passed. The tears flowed as I recognized my truth. I did try to "save" him.

Roland reached into his pile of Purple Papers and pulled mine out. It felt like such a gift to me. It was five days after my birthday. To receive confirmation that Jay knew what was in my heart and how I did all I could with the limits that were placed on me at the time was incredibly healing. I know he's in a better place, and the comforting message I received from him eased my pain. It helped me feel free to know he believed in me, in the healing I was doing and in God's love and the promise of peace. My prayer for him was peace and Roland affirmed his daily prayer for peace as well.

His message, written next to a drawing of him in bed bathed in golden light, said, "My head doesn't hurt. We tried everything to get me better. I know how much you tried to save me—day after day I prayed for peace."

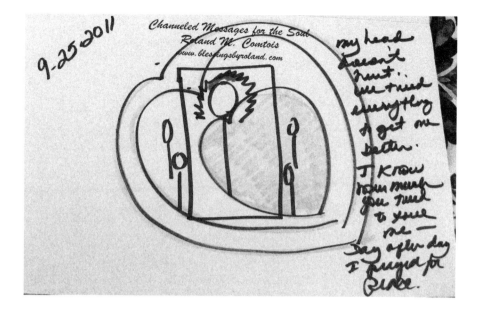

It doesn't take away the heartache or grief or void in our family, but it reminds me that our loved ones live on in the afterlife, and it affirms the power of eternal love for us all.

Chapter 39

CIRCLE OF LOVE
BY DAWN L. ROSA

Five days after Paul passed, I was driving home from work and saw his face. It appeared before me almost like that of a ghost in a smoky fog. I wasn't sure what to make of it at the time, but I now believe that he wanted me to see him for the last time. Or perhaps he wanted to see me for the last time.

Paul was my one true love. He was the one who opened my heart to receive, understand, and allow love in. You see, I was an abused and neglected child. Growing up, I never knew what love was nor did I realize it even existed. When Paul came into my life, he changed all that. He changed everything. He changed me.

We met when I was a sophomore in high school. Paul was a handsome, sweet, and a very kind high school senior. He was patient, compassionate, and caring and made me feel like I was the most important person in the world. He was beyond special, almost heaven sent. Our souls connected, and I wanted to spend the rest of my life with him. He felt the same way. We were inseparable for almost a year until he went into the service. Prior to going into basic training, he proposed to me. I accepted with all my heart, knowing without question that we were destined to be together forever. While he was away, we wrote to each other daily, not letting a single day go by without reaching out to one another, telling stories, sharing dreams, sending love. But our story didn't have the happily-ever-after ending I longed for. When Paul returned home from the service, he was a very different man, changed perhaps by what he experienced serving our country. I was different too. Add the fact that his mother couldn't bear the thought of living apart from him and asked him to choose between her and me, and our relationship ended before I knew it. Blood is thicker than water, they say. When push came to shove, Paul chose his mom and I was left with a broken heart.

Time went by, wounds healed, and we each married someone else and started our own families. Our paths crossed years later when I ran into him and learned he was going through an ugly divorce. I almost gave him my number in the event he needed a friend, but I decided against it. I was married with a family, and I wasn't all that sure I could trust myself around him. He was suffering then, way beyond what I had seen or even imagined. Visitation rights to his children were being withheld. He was depressed and distraught and started drinking. I didn't know any of this. Thoughts of Paul faded into the rhythm of everyday life until one day, out of the blue, I received a call from a longtime friend saying Paul had died. Died? My heart skipped a beat. I couldn't breathe. But how? Why? Oh God, no. Not Paul. Not my Paul. I found out he took his life with his own hands. I was heartbroken, crushed, horrified. I reeled with the very real pain of never seeing him again. What happened? Could I have done something to help?

I received answers to my questions on the Purple Papers that Roland gave to me during his presentations. On the first one, Roland had drawn a table and two end chairs. There were a lot of dots on the table. I had no idea what it meant, but somehow I realized this paper wasn't for me. It belonged to someone else; it was meant for Paul's mother. I had made amends with her at Paul's funeral when we came together in our grief, forgiving her for asking her son to make a choice between us. As the mother of two boys now, I finally understood the motivation behind her actions so many years ago. A mother at the tender age of sixteen, she was a child herself when she had Paul and literally grew up with him. She only wanted the best for son and thought she alone could provide it. I realized what she did back then, she did out of love for him. She didn't know the ramifications that choice would have on her son or me. I could see how devastated she was by her loss, as was I. We tried to help each other through the pain. I made peace with her for her sake, for Paul, for me.

I brought that Purple Paper home and tucked it into a box in my closet, deciding that it wasn't the right time to give it to his mother. I would bring it to her when she was strong enough to see it. That time came on its own, when one day I found it lying on the closet floor, with the door open so I could easily see it. I hadn't taken it out of the box. "Who did?" I asked myself as I put it back where I had been keeping it. Days later, the closet door opened again. What was this about? Then it hit me that I needed to bring this paper to his mother. She cried when I handed it to her. She knew immediately what it meant. Through her tears, she explained that the table and chairs at Paul's house looked exactly like the ones drawn on the Purple Paper. Same placement, same setting, same everything. The dots we saw? They were the pills that Paul took that ended his life. There were so many he hadn't taken them all. His mother told me there were still pills on the table when Paul was found.

Years later I met Roland again and received another Purple Paper. Roland had written the message as he received from Paul. It said, "He's sorry he didn't take you to the last dance." That last dance would have been our wedding dance. Roland remembered seeing an altar when he wrote that down. I wasn't surprised. I had never stopped loving him, and I believe he felt the same way too.

Messages from Paul kept coming. He said, "I thought this out for a minute—I couldn't get my head around it anymore. I didn't plan anything." Another Purple Paper years later read, "Paul spent the last two weeks really nervous about his illness. Four days before he passed, he knew there was nothing else to do. You did alright," referring I believe to my decision not to give him my number when we ran into one another during his divorce.

1/18/2011

Channeled Messages for the Soul
Roland M. Comtois
401-647-4446
www.blessingsbyroland.com

I thought this out for a minute — I couldn't get my head around it anymore. I didn't plan anything.

3-14-2015

Roland M. Comtois - The Purple Paper
Channeled Messages for the Soul
www.blessingsbyroland.com

No more doctor visits YAY!

Paul spent the last two weeks really nervous about his illness. Four days before he passed he knew there was nothing else to do. You did alright!

Another paper read, "Paul didn't see his life changing. Everything was moving so fast. When I passed away, I saw my grandmother (and Mary). Wow! This stuff is so real!!!"

Roland M. Comtois - *The Purple Papers*
Channeled Messages for the Soul
www.blessingsbyroland.com

10-20-2015

Paul didn't see life changing. Everything was moving so fast. When I passed away I saw my grandmother (+ mary). wow! This stuff is so real!!!

He wanted me to know that I "deserve true love" in another paper: "Paul stopped telling you what he was going through, so how would you know (he says)? I wanted you to be mine forever. I wanted you to know that you do deserve true love."

Roland M. Comtois - *The Purple Papers*
Channeled Messages for the Soul
www.blessingsbyroland.com

8.4.2015

Paul stopped telling you what he was going through, so how would you know (he says). I wanted you to be mine forever. I wanted you to know that you do deserve true love.

Our love for one another was and still is so strong. After he passed away, all the letters I wrote to him while he was in the service were found. He had saved them for the past twenty years. He's still writing to me from heaven, filling my heart and soul with the knowledge that love is unending and eternal.

My life and love for Paul have come full circle. The experiences we shared on earth and from heaven led me to a place where dreams and possibilities live, where second chances are freely given, where past transgressions are truly forgiven, and where love never ever dies.

Chapter 40

LOVE, DADDY
BY KAITLYN BOUCHARD DICICCO

When I was eleven years old, my best friend suddenly passed away. He was my dad and only thirty-seven years old. I couldn't understand what had happened. How could life be so cruel? My parents were divorced, and I only got to see him every other weekend, but we had so much fun together. Go-karts, mini golf, amusement parks, late-night snack runs—memories I'll never forget. They were extra special since I was an only child.

My dad meant the world to me, and I longed to know if he was OK. Was there really a heaven? Is his spirit still around me? Has he been watching me grow up? Am I making him proud? In February 2010, almost eight years after my dad passed, my mom and I went to see Roland at an event. I was skeptical and nervous about going and almost backed out. I'm so glad I went, because that night really had a profound impact on my life.

My dad came through. A lot. It was insane. Toward the beginning of the night, Roland looked at me and said, "He keeps yelling 'Kaitlyn,' trying to get through." Then Roland kept looking me in the eye saying, "I love you, I love you, I love you, you're still mine, I love you, I love you." At one point, Roland was on the other side of the room talking to someone else, and then he stopped midsentence, walked over to me, and said, "Where's the heart? You have the heart—it's in your pocketbook." Then he went back to talking to the other person. Not even my mom knew I had brought the gold heart necklace with my dad's face on it. It has "always in my heart" written on the back of it.

Later on, Roland went around the room and talked to everyone, and once he came back to me, he said, "Where's the heart?" I handed him the necklace and he looked a little confused. He then said, "Where's the pink heart?" I was confused for a second, but then I gasped, remembering that I brought a card Dad had handmade for me when I was little. It said, "To my very special little girl," and on the inside was a giant pink heart that said "Happy Valentine's Day" and "I will be home very soon. Be a good girl for Mommy. Love, Daddy." Everyone there was in disbelief.

Roland asked what I put in my dad's pockets. I had Father's Day gifts I was planning to give to him that I put in there. Roland acted like my dad when he spoke: "He's a young guy, a character." At one point he called me Katie—my dad was the only one who called me that.

Later that night, Roland presented me with a Purple Paper he had drawn on December 15, 2009. It was a drawing of the gold necklace with the words "I've been with you for so long." It also had the date "12/03" written on it, which at first I thought meant December, but I recently realized that my aunt gave me the gold necklace in December 2003.

That night and experience with Roland gave me some closure on the loss of my dad. It meant the world to me to know that he is OK and is with me every step of the way. Since losing him, I've helped many others with their own losses and even won an award for a film I made that honored my dad. I will never forget that night and the comfort it's brought me every day since then.

In October 2017, devastating family circumstances brought me to seek out spiritual guidance. I learned that Roland was having an event, so I went with my mom and my aunt (my dad's sister).

During a break, I was getting my photo taken with my 2010 Purple Paper for consideration for this book. Roland asked me who it was from. I said my dad. He asked how long he's been gone. I told him fifteen years. He asked for his name and if I thought he had any more messages for me. I said, "His name is Kevin and I hope so."

Then he looked over my shoulder and said, "Oh! He's here right now! You're here because you want to know what to do next."

After the event, Roland said, "I want to go over there and talk to that girl about her dad." He came over to me and said, "He's been gone a long time, and he's not here to talk about him being dead. It's about your family." He went on to say, "I wish it wasn't so complicated. It wasn't easy to live, easy to die, or easy to stay. I still left too soon."

He asked if I was a mother. I said, "Yes, my son is four months old."

Roland said, "He's talking about a baby. He met him. He was there. He met all the kids. He says he would have been a good grandfather."

I only have one child so far, so this statement makes me think that my dad has met my future children as well. Roland also said, "He's moving you along, guiding you, encouraging you. You're brave." Later on, Roland spoke with me, my mom, and my aunt and showed us a Purple Paper. He wasn't sure if it was about my dad or not. The paper said, "Kevin loved life, his family and friends. I did get very, very sick fast. I found so much peace from all of you. During my last day, I knew I had to go. I'm good because of you."

The paper also said he was adventurous and he died at home before making it to the hospital. My dad died suddenly while at home alone vacuuming. He was cleaning his house and even got a nice suit out. It's like he knew. He even told my mom a couple days before to take care of me. The day he died he had an appointment at the hospital to see if he needed open heart surgery. He died before he could make it to the appointment. This paper was definitely from my dad. It gave me, my mom, and my aunt so much comfort. Roland also said to my mom that my dad "wasn't her ex," that she was "his one and only." Most people would be surprised to hear this, but those who knew him well knew how much he loved my mom even after their divorce.

In November 2017, my mom and I went to the Mind Body Spirit Expo. We bought a couple of Roland's books and had him sign them. He asked, "Can I write what I hear?" We said yes, and he wrote, "I will always be there for you. I will always look out for you. Dad." In my mom's book, he wrote "You were right." Then he started saying "Kevin" without us telling him anything.

Later on at the expo, Roland gave a talk, and my dad came through again. A lot. "Don't you think your father wants to whisper in your ear one more time? Don't you think your father wants to give you more courage and strength, and don't you think he's been holding you together in some way? 'Cause that's why you're here. You're here for the entire audience to stand by your side. I'm asking everyone who can hear me to stand by this woman's side as her father gives her a moment of hope. You have come here for all of us to embrace you in some way. Your father has been standing there with you on your path. Helping you. And your father wants me to tell you for the last four and a half months that he's been holding you together. Your father wants me to embrace you like you're my own kid and he wants to talk with you about life and the experiences you've been going through. He says you feel him already, and he's so happy that you've done so well in your life."

Roland begins clapping, and then the entire audience starts clapping for me. "Your father is holding you with all the love that he has." These messages from my dad mean the world to me as I'm going through the most difficult time in my life. Knowing that he's by my side gives me hope that things will be resolved soon.

Chapter 41

THE CAKE TOPPER
BY DANDAYA MELIA

I lost both of my parents not long after I met the man I was going to marry. Their deaths left me shaken and unsure of how to move forward in my life. I longed for their counsel and blessings, so when I learned about one of Roland's Channeled Messages for the Soul events in Woonsocket, Rhode Island, I decided I would go. I really wanted to get a message from them. But I was also very nervous. Will my dad come? Is my mom OK? Will I get a message? What if I don't get a message? Does that mean they have forgotten me or that they don't care? Are they happy? Should I get married? Does my dad like him?

The questions, doubts, and insecurities raced through my mind and body, adding to my fears about my upcoming wedding. My fiancé and I had been engaged for thirteen years before we finally set the date. I loved him with all my heart, but I worried about who was going to walk me down the aisle in my father's place. It seems silly now, but back then it was paralyzing.

As the day of the event arrived, I made sure I had something of my father's and a bracelet of my mother's with me, hoping that these personal items would help me get a message. When I got in my car to leave that day, I remember looking at the time to make sure I wouldn't be late. It was 3:21 p.m.

When I arrived at the venue where Roland was speaking, I felt a chill as we entered the room. I shrugged it off as I wrote my name, Dandaya, on the nametags we were given. I sat down in the chairs that were lined up in rows and waited for Roland to start.

As he walked in and started talking to the people who were there, he said, "Angela's parents are here." My parents called me Angela, I remember thinking, but there is no way Roland could know that. When I let him know that he might be referring to me, he came over to me and shared messages that I knew could only be from my mother and dad. Roland even took on my mother's Asian personality as he spoke.

My parents had divorced when I was in my teens and because of it, my mother and I did not get along well. In fact, four days before she died, she wasn't speaking to me. It was right after the tragic Station nightclub fire in Warwick, Rhode Island on February 20, 2003. I had driven past the site the next day against her wishes and it had made her upset. She had a massive stroke on February 25 and died in my old bedroom before we had a chance to speak to one another again.

Through Roland, my mother said that she loved me very much and was proud of me. She said, "It wasn't your fault. I was looking for someone to blame," no doubt referring to the rift we experienced after the divorce. A heavy weight was lifted off my heart. Two weeks later I learned that I was pregnant with my daughter. She was due on my mom's birthday.

Then Roland asked me if I was getting married. I nodded a yes. That's when he gave me my first Purple Paper. It had a sketch on it of the wedding cake topper I had just purchased, with two hearts joined together. It was the second cake topper I had purchased. The first one I had bought had a date on it and we couldn't use it because our date had to be changed.

The message on that paper was from my father, who assured me that he would be there at my wedding: "I know the secret code. Yes, I will be at your wedding. I wouldn't miss it for the world. You two belong together." My fears immediately vanished as I realized that my dad had answered my questions—and my prayers. I was relieved and elated. I had the closure I needed to move on.

I heard that Roland was coming to town again to participate in an event that was being held at a convention venue where I had purchased my wedding dress. The date of the event was the anniversary of my dad's death. They were holding a drawing for free tickets, and the winners' names would be posted on Facebook. That's where I learned that I won a ticket.

I found Roland's booth in the exact same spot where the wedding dress vendor had been located a year before. I couldn't help but think that all the coincidences that were occurring that day were signs. It wasn't until I saw a photo of my Purple Paper from my dad displayed in Roland's booth that I knew without a doubt that my dad was somehow behind all of this.

While I was there, Roland's daughter told me that the Purple Papers Roland had been using were now in a lighter purple color. She mentioned the time frame that this color switch occurred, and I quickly realized that it occurred at the same time that I ordered my daughter's flower girl dress, which was the exact color shade of the paper!

I received my second Purple Paper on Roland's Facebook page. It was dated on the same day as my mother's birthday. This message was again from my father. He told Roland to tell me, "I really did my best here. I know sometimes it was hard for you, but honestly, I'm OK now. No more pressures, no more headaches, no more worries." He finished his message with "I love you so much" and left his name on the paper, Daniel. It also said, "P.S. Look for the signs." In addition to all those coincidences that had occurred since that very first Purple Paper message, the entire week before I received this message, I felt his presence so strongly.

My father had been bedridden before he passed, suffering with multiple sclerosis, PTSD, and constant headaches. His legs had given out too, but his spirit was always upbeat and caring. He didn't want me to worry and I remember him telling me that he would never leave me until he knew I had found someone to take care of me. He met my husband a few weeks after we had started dating and told me how much he liked him. He died a few weeks later of a massive heart attack. When he was found, he had been clutching a photo of him and me to his heart.

On my wedding day, six minutes before I was to walk down the aisle, the rain stopped and the sun came out. It had been pouring for hours before, with no sign that the weather would let up for my ceremony. When the gate opened and I began my walk down the aisle toward my husband and our wedding guests, a heart appeared on my arm. It is clearly visible in that first wedding photo.

I needn't have worried about my wedding for all those years after my father died. My father was there with me always, and he did walk me down the aisle at my wedding, sharing a love that's truly heaven sent and eternally blessed.

Chapter 42

I GOT THE MESSAGE

BY LINA L. LEBRUN

The first time I saw Roland was at a little Spiritualist church in Onset, Massachusetts. I did not receive a personal message that day, but I was most impressed with Roland. His words were so sincere and meaningful that people were crying at other people's messages. I thought then how comforting it was to learn that your loved ones in spirit were there watching over and loving you and that they had made their way to a place we call heaven. And how people of all faiths and ages came together to support others in their grief and newfound peace.

When I had the opportunity to see Roland again, I actually never thought I would get a Purple Paper from my mother! The evening arrived and Roland came up to me right away. He began by saying things that we all recognized as my mother's words—the way he spoke even sounded like her. She talked about many things through Roland, not the least of which was her adamant refusal to go into a nursing home. My mother told us time and time again how she felt about going into a nursing home and even insinuated that she had made plans to end her own life if the day came when she would be unable to care for herself and, as she put it, "be a burden to others." If this were not evidence enough that she made her presence known that night, Roland even declared the exact date that she had crossed over! I was in shock.

When Roland was again in my area, I purchased tickets to the show. During the event he addressed me directly and asked me when my mother had passed. I was very surprised that he asked me a direct question without giving me a message; he instead asked me to come to see him after the event. What was that all about, I wondered? I had read about Purple Papers; I had even seen people receiving them at the last event! Could it possibly be that there was one for me in his stack of precious messages? For the remainder of the evening, I was torn between paying attention to the messages being delivered and the anticipation of what was going to happen later.

My prayers were answered, and Roland did have a Purple Paper for me. The message had been written in August 2009, and there, two years later, I was receiving it in August 2011. My Purple Paper read, "I left on 4-14 with no chance to get free." It has a big heart in the center. Roland later added, "I know you did it so well. Difficulty. (I'm sorry.)"

I have wondered what she meant by saying, "I know you did it so well." Originally, I had thought she was referring to getting free from a body that was no longer serving her, but how did that relate to me?

As I was writing this, a full six years after receiving my precious Purple Paper, I had a much-delayed aha moment.

My mother worked very hard and did so much for us: cooking, cleaning, sewing, chauffeuring, etc. All hems were perfectly even and bangs were always straight. Everything always looked really good, but there were no hugs or *I love you*s from my hardworking mom. I do not know what had happened to her in her past, but she was not an emotionally present woman.

Fortunately for me, my great aunt and godmother lived next door, and she, despite having lost all three of her children in their early childhood, was still able to connect with me as a young child. We were very close, and she was my emotional mother. One day, when I was seven years old, I came home from school and found my beloved Tante Clementine dead on the floor of her kitchen. She was blue. I was devastated and I shut down emotionally. I essentially became my mother from an emotional standpoint.

The spirit world has its ways of letting you know what you need, and soon after her death, a visitor who came to me on several occasions within a year or two after that. The spirit had the form of a man who was dressed in the fashions of the early 1900s. I was not at all frightened, and we communicated. I never thought of it then, but it must have been telepathically. One day, my spirit visitor told me that he would not be returning and that was his final visit. I asked his name, and what my seven-year-old brain remembered from that conversation was "Mr. Benson." For decades later, I fondly remembered the visits from Mr. Benson. It gave me something to hang on to as I had emotionally encased myself in what I described as a ten-foot thick block of ice. Mr. Benson and the memory of my beloved aunt were the rays of light that kept me from freezing over completely in my self-imposed block of ice.

In addition to doing a lot of work in self-help programs, I sought out readings from mediums and past-life visionaries. I also became interested in genealogy. All of these helped me gradually melt my block of ice and also helped me identify who my Mr. Benson was. From old photos that were generously gifted to me from relatives, my genealogy research and confirmation from spirit messages, I am quite confident in identifying my Mr. Benson as my great uncle Benjamin, an older brother of my emotional mother, Tante Clementine.

After all these years, I believe that I finally do understand the meaning behind my mother's message on my Purple Paper. In life, she was never able to free herself from her emotional bondage, and I have been able to do so, at least in part, and with great "difficulty."

I get the message now, Mom.

Chapter 43

SEASHELLS

BY BOBBI PARLETT

I met Roland during my grief journey following the passing of my husband, Ed. He had passed after a five-month battle with bladder cancer in the middle of the night after experiencing breathing problems. I know now that my husband, who was quite skeptical about the afterlife, let alone the possibility of any kind of communication between heaven and earth, is still in my life. My story is even more poignant since he didn't believe in mediums or the possibility of communicating after death.

It was March 2013, when my sister, also a widow, noting my state of numbness in my grief and trying to figure it all out, invited me to a conference that focused on grief and the afterlife. Roland was one of the speakers at the upcoming June conference. In the presence of about one hundred and fifty people, Roland talked about our loved ones and how they remained with us. He picked me out of the crowd and told me that my husband was standing behind me. He moved quickly to a woman sitting in another row and told her that her son was with her, and then just as fast, he told another lady that her mother was with her. He then proceeded to give specific messages to various people in the audience, eliciting tears at times, laughter at others, and often gasps of surprise. Some of these messages came through prewritten on the Purple Papers he carried with him to the conference.

Roland came back to me several times as he shared messages from my husband. He said my husband knew how hard I tried to do what I could to make him feel better, and that "the fear was gone" now. "My wife needs to know I had trouble breathing but I found peace."

He also said, "I found Dad," especially meaningful because my father had passed away suddenly on the same day, years earlier, as my husband. Without question, I could relate to all these messages. Given my husband's dismissal of this kind of thing during his lifetime, I was in awe that I actually received a message. And I was beyond happy that my husband communicated with me. The people in the room were equally engaged, sharing in the energy and experiences as if they were the ones receiving the message. Whether they were blessed with one or not, everyone in the room left with a feeling of hope, love, and peace. I know I did.

Two years later, I helped plan an event for Roland in Hilton Head, South Carolina. The day before the event, Roland and I had a few minutes to chat. I mentioned that I wanted to go to the beach to look for seashells because I loved to collect shells. Roland paused with a curious look in his eyes and said that he had written a Purple Paper about a seashell collection. He had it among the stacks of Purple Papers he carries with him. I was curious about the possibility of it being for me. He said he would have to look at it and see if he felt that the message was for me or not. At the end of that evening's event, Roland gave out many Purple Papers for people in attendance, all recorded well in advance without him knowing whom they were meant for. I held my breath before learning that I was one of them. He handed me the Purple Paper he had told me about earlier that day, the one with the seashell collection message.

I looked at the date that was written on the paper, since it is oftentimes significant to the story being told. I racked my brain trying to figure out the meaning of that date to me. Why was it important? Where had I been that day? Was this paper really for me? Then I remembered I had visited my granddaughter that day and had brought with me the seashells we had collected together on a recent trip to Florida. We made a stepping-stone out of them, putting the shells in concrete to preserve them forever.

On the Purple Paper Roland had written the words he had heard from beyond: "Why don't you start a seashell collection?" Roland noted that as he was writing the message, he heard laughter and felt joy, and a whispered after comment of "Just what you need, another collection." My husband had a dry sense of humor, so this comment was more than right on! "I send them to you. Do you know why? Just to tell you I'm right here."

Roland M. Comtois - *The Purple Papers*
Channeled Messages for the Soul
www.blessingsbyroland.com

6-6-2015

Why don't you start a "sea shell collection?" (heard laughter-felt joy). Just what you need another collection. I send them to you. Do you know why? Just to tell you, I'm right here

After Roland's event, I went to see my granddaughter and the stepping-stone and took a picture of it. At home, I again looked at the Purple Paper and noticed that Roland had drawn water on the paper and a heart in the bottom right corner. I had to catch my breath. The stepping-stone that my granddaughter and I made, on the same day that Roland wrote the Purple Paper, was in the shape of a heart!

Ed and I met in the Bahamas on a little island called Exuma, where we both happened to be vacationing. In love with the amazing seashells I always found there, I also fell in love with the amazing man I met there. After we were married, we returned often, where I still collected seashells on every visit. My husband would laugh, asking me what I was going to do with all those seashells. I smiled, saying I would think of something. After he passed,

I would take the kids and grandchildren to Florida, where I continued to collect seashells by the shore.

Through Roland's Purple Paper, I was overwhelmed that my husband had been with my granddaughter and me as we worked on that heart-shaped stepping-stone and that he wanted us to know he was with us and knew what we were doing!

My experiences at Roland's events have been major factors in my ability to move forward with my life, in the deepening of my spirituality, and in the strengthening of my understanding of the afterlife. I am comforted to know that my beloved husband is always with me in spirit and that our love is everlasting.

Chapter 44

NO MORE JUDGMENT

BY KARYNE JOHNSON

I grew up in northern California, immersed, ensconced, and inexorably in-
doctrinated in the Mormon culture that my father, and generations of his
family before him, had adopted unquestionably as their chosen faith. It was a
doctrine passionately promulgated by zealous missionaries who enticed my
great-grandparents from Scotland to America in the late 1800s to begin their
lives anew under the tenets of a religion that gave them privileged access to a
promised land of plenty, "safe from ridicule and strife," in a community of
like-minded fellow "Saints." For all intents and purposes, "Saint" should be
the operative word here, because even as a little girl growing up in a house-
hold hell-bent on adhering to the teachings of its prophets more than a hundred years after my great-grandparents' conversion, I was fully expected to
be a saint. Truth be told, I was anything but. And the promise of living in a
place safe from ridicule and strife? That too proved to be a lifelong contradic-
tion for me.

Being a member of the Mormon Church of Jesus Christ of the Latter-day
Saints meant conforming to ideals, rules, and regulations that dictated
one's every thought and action. I resisted them for as long as I could
remember. I was spirited and outspoken, more apt to challenge

authority than acquiesce to it. I was put off by rigid thinking and dreamed of a life full of adventure and creative fulfillment. I longed to be appreciated and accepted for who I was and what I believed in. And perhaps more than anything else, I wanted my father, a pillar of the Church and the patriarch of our family and Mormon community, to be proud of me and not the saint I was expected to be.

My father cut an impressive figure. An MBA graduate of Palo Alto's cerebral Stanford University, he was sophisticated and refined, highly intelligent, endlessly motivated, and a born leader. He excelled in high school, both academically and socially, parlaying his redheaded good looks and affable personality into easily won elections as class and club president. In spite of his rarely talked about, challenging undergraduate years at college, "Red," as he was fondly known as by friends and colleagues, went on to serve a distinguished tour of duty in Naval Intelligence and further his education while a newlywed.

The firstborn, I came along when my father was on the fast track to success at school, with dreams of climbing the corporate ladder at AT&T. That he had wanted a son became apparent to me as I grew up in the shadow of his disappointment. Having a son was more than a point of pride for Mormon men like my father. A son meant that their legacy of leadership would be passed on for eternity. Daughters could never hold that priesthood position in the Church, could never attain the status and power that separated them from the laypeople in their congregations. Daughters could not become the "gods" the men aspired to be. So I never could be good enough or smart enough to live up to his expectations no matter how hard I tried. He may have faulted me for being a girl, but he couldn't deny that I was persistent and dogged in my determination to be an independent, intelligent thinker like him.

But that may have been my downfall in his eyes.

By the time I was three years old, the Mormon Church would become his family and his all-consuming mission. He had rallied against it for years as a rebellious young adult, questioning its rules, defying its restrictions, and flaunting his predilection for fun and frat parties. But then a "revelation" changed everything. Now, as a husband and father, he found Mormonism not only embracing but empowering. He would spend the rest of his life persuasively espousing its virtues and sharing its message. Just as he soared to the highest executive ranks at AT&T, he rose to the influential, hugely powerful positions of bishop and state president in charge of eight congregations, charming and cajoling his flock with promises of eternal rewards for a life lived well according to prevailing Mormon ideals. I alone remained an unconverted bane in his mission.

Listening to him denounce the lifestyle sins of a non-Mormon world, I was not convinced that his way was the right way. I wanted more, more opportunities to learn, grow, evolve. I wanted the freedom to follow my dreams and my spiritual path to become the woman I knew I was. I didn't want to be subservient or self-dismissing like my fellow Mormon sisters. I couldn't remain demure and deny my desires. I did not want to defer to a man, father, or husband. Mormons have a mission to spread the word about their eternal kingdom. I was a girl on a mission, all right, but not the Church's mission. As far as my father was concerned, I was a rebel, and he spent our years together trying to change that.

Because of our opposing views on life and the Church, our relationship became more and more strained as I experienced more of life. I know he loved me, yet I feared him. He demanded perfection. I sought reality. He wanted me to fit into a mold. I wanted to break out of it. He discouraged my dating non-Mormon boys, and I found them much more interesting and fun than my Church-endorsed counterparts.

We did share a love of lovely things. A gifted writer, he taught me to appreciate poetry and classical music. We both admired fine antiques, were passionate about interior design, and held fast to our unwavering beliefs in self-sufficiency and free enterprise. That was our bond, our special connection, and I always remained grateful to him for teaching me to embrace the sensibilities and elegant refinements that define my life today. Sadly, the Church created a life-long schism between us that we couldn't seem to overlook or overcome.

I realized early on that the best way to keep peace with my father was to stay under the radar, in conversation, in actions, and in all outward appearances. So while I appeased him by attending Brigham Young University, the college he and the Church chose for all good Mormons—especially for young women, whom it was generally understood would bring home a "returned missionary husband" along with their degree—once I was away from home, I started to think for myself in earnest. I had to adhere to a proper dress code under the threat of expulsion: no pants on campus, no sleeveless tops, prim attire at all times. But I shortened my hems when I took off for off-campus parties and dances where rock music, banned from campus life, liberated feelings unnaturally and forcibly repressed by the Church-run University, and tried to buck the system whenever I could.

I did come home engaged to someone I met in college, but my father was more than disappointed in my choice of life partner. I remember how he and my mother tried to do all they could to derail our relationship. That only furthered my resolve. I was married in a traditional ceremony in the Mormon Temple, secretly chafing under the required temple garments and restrictions imposed on me, albeit determined to be the best, most perfect wife I could be. Our union, ostensibly sealed for eternity, was tumultuous and trying. It lasted eleven years, produced two beautiful children, and took me to the East Coast, far from the Mormon stronghold I grew up in.

As my marriage unraveled, so too did my ties to the Church. My father's controlling comments, once so strongly Church oriented, morphed into personal criticisms and judgments about my parenting, my career, my looks, my life choices. Behind my back, he tried to bribe my children into helping him bring me and our little family back to the Church so we wouldn't be "cast out into the darkness." It never worked.

Our last face-to-face conversation took place six months before he died and more than forty years after I left my father's house as a married woman and traveled cross-country to start a new life. I flew out to California for my obligatory biannual visit, as always making sure my hair, clothes, and makeup were perfect before seeing him. I worried needlessly about whether I had gained that extra pound or two that my father would unfailingly and critically point out on my already model thin body, and I nervously anticipated whether I would measure up to the high standards and judgments that had plagued me all my life. Here I was, a successful career woman and the mother of two amazingly accomplished grown children, and yet I felt as vulnerable and insecure as I did when I was a little girl.

My father looked frail and beaten down by taking care of my Alzheimer's-stricken mother, but his spirit was as strong as ever. He couldn't let go of the fact that I had rejected his beloved faith, his spiritual laws. He implored me to return to the Church.

"I wish you would reconsider coming back to the Church," he said as I bid him goodbye. "I don't want to lose you and your family for all eternity."

He unexpectedly passed away a few months later, never reconciling with the decisions I made about my life. I was sorry that he had never given me the emotional support and unconditional love I needed while he was alive and regretted the many father-daughter opportunities and conversations we missed. Was I ever worthy in his eyes? It's amazing how much we crave affirmation from our loved ones, how their actions and words affect us on the deepest levels. I shuddered at the thought of carrying that burden with me for the rest of my days.

I sought out spiritual guidance rather than organized religion to find inner peace, taking comfort in the knowledge of the existence of a higher power and the possibility of messages from the other side. That's how I found myself at one of Roland's Channeled Messages for the Soul presentations in November 2008, not knowing what to expect but hoping for something nonetheless. What I received was more priceless than I could have ever imagined and set in a motion a series of "revelations" that have made all the difference for me in how I viewed my father.

Other than the hostess, I didn't know any of the people in the room that day. I looked around at the men and women, young and old, who perched expectantly on the folding chairs that had been set out in a semicircle and took note of the boxes of tissues that had been strategically placed in between them. Then Roland walked into the room with a disclaimer about the experience we were about to embark on, saying that the messages some of us were about to receive may not be what we expected but that they would be exactly what we needed to hear.

He moved from person to person quickly, stopping to hold a hand, offer an embrace, examine a ring, share a story. His mannerisms took on the persona of loved ones communicating from beyond, arms crossed here, fingers pointing there, soothing touches reminiscent of tender partings, laughter, tears. His presence was riveting, his messages poignant and personal for the recipients. I held my breath as he walked over to me.

"Your father's here. He said he is sorry for being so rigid and he has come to terms with the reality of spirit and religion. He had a spiritual awakening and he wants me to tell you …" Roland's voice broke off in midsentence as he bounded to the front of the room to retrieve a large Purple Paper that had a map of the United States drawn on it with an arrow pointing from Connecticut to San Francisco. "This is for you," he said. "Your father wants me to "tell my daughter that I am sorry she had to do so much traveling to California for the estate." And there was something else on it, a message written inside the outline of map:

"Tell my daughter she should feel OK—no guilt—no restlessness—OK—OK."

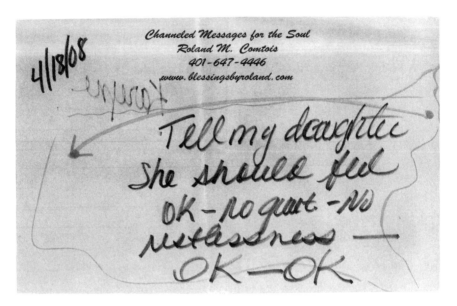

It was dated April 2008. My father had passed away the first week in February. Since then, I had flown to California no fewer than five times, overwhelmed at having to deal with the exhausting cross-country flights, the stress and emotions that choked my every thought, the stacks and stacks of papers and receipts that overflowed from his desk and files. I was astounded that Roland had picked up on this and that my father knew how difficult these trips had been for me. Then there was that telltale expression my father was fond of repeating: OK, OK. When I read those two words, I actually heard his voice and knew at once it was, and could only be, a message from my father.

I saw Roland next a year later at a large group presentation in a historic mansion in Norwalk, Connecticut, when he had another Purple Paper message for me. It was dated March 26, 2009, and on it was the apology I waited a lifetime to hear.

"You were right. I was wrong."

Bingo! I knew instantly what this meant. My father finally recognized and allowed me my spiritual quest and knew he had been wrong to force feed me the Mormon teachings.

"Your father is here," said Roland as he handed the paper to me. There was a big desk drawn on the paper with piles of papers on it. I recognized it immediately as my father's. There was the unmistakable 1940s stapler with the rounded top that my father always kept on the desk, next to the leather pen and pencil cup. And the stacks and stacks of papers were placed exactly as I remembered them. It was an indelible icon from my childhood and Roland had portrayed the entire image as if he had seen it with his own eyes. It was a picture that needed no explanation. My jaw dropped. The paper read, "I'm sorry I left you with all the papers."

"He wants me to tell you that 'the vision of how you want to live your life and see your future is right. Keep going,'" Roland said.

I nodded, eyes glistening with unbidden tears, as I reached for the tissue I found being handed to me. There was no doubt that my father had sent these messages. I could feel my soul, my heart, start to heal.

There were to be four Purple Paper messages in all from my father to me, prerecorded and dated by Roland to reflect the day they were received and written.

When we next met, Roland sought me out in the crowd. "I have been waiting to deliver this message to the right person," said Roland, clearly confused by the name written on the paper. It was dated March 30, 2009. He handed it to me, saying, "I think this is for you." I gasped out loud as I read it.

Written on it were the words "Roland has found his way to a place of comfort."

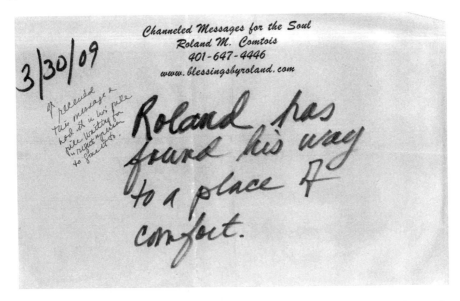

The name Roland, my father's name, was outlined in red. Red was his nickname, due to his red hair and his initials, R. E. D. Never in my discussions with Roland Comtois had my father's name or nickname ever come up. The red outline around it erased any doubt about its origin and blew me away. Throughout his life, largely because of the unrelenting pressures and indoctrination by the Mormon Church, my father strived for perfection, always reaching for idealized goals that were unattainable here on earth. His expectations of me as his daughter were no less demanding and unrealistic.

To know that a man so tortured in life had now found a place where he could relax and find comfort in just being himself was more than I could hope for. I breathed a liberating sigh of relief and experienced a lightness I had never known before. I had grown up with the notion that love was conditional and now, thanks to Roland's Purple Papers, I knew that true love, eternal love, was freely given, no strings attached. His messages took away all the barriers and judgments that had existed between me and my father, absolved me from the self-defeating pain and anguish I had lived with for decades and wiped it all out, just like that.

Everything dovetailed when I received the last of the Purple Paper messages from my father, dated April 11, 2009. "Your father says he owes you this," Roland told me.

"Owes no more judgment." These simple words written on purple paper had the power to change everything and instill the forgiveness I never imagined possible.

LOVE UNCLAIMED: THE PURPLE PAPERS YET TO BE DELIVERED

The stories in this book began with Purple Papers that I delivered to those who needed them most. From sacred etchings depicting life stories to words that fuel healing, the Purple Papers for decades have confirmed the existence of love everlasting and the validity of the afterlife.

I've had daily conversations with people who have passed. They share their untold personal stories of life lived and love shared, entrusting me with messages for the loved ones left behind. I record them on my Purple Papers so one day I can reunite them with the person for whom it was written.

A young woman longs for her dad to stand strong and speak to her once again. A daughter of an aging mother carries out her mom's wishes precisely as prescribed. A forgotten love is re-experienced through the ethers of the universal connection. Each predocumented Purple Paper message offers the witness an opportunity to push through doubt and disbelief about life beyond.

For years, I have sat in front of the blank Purple Papers, hoping that what they say and what they represent becomes a revelation that touches the heart of those who experience them. Because to touch one heart in one moment of time reawakens the humanity in all of us. It is a magnificent discovery when one Purple Paper reaches far beyond the one for whom it is inscribed and resonates unexpectedly with a stranger. A gasp. The quiet rush of tears and awe that surface when one Purple Paper is delivered.

Time and time again, I have dated and prewritten every Purple Paper message, long before seeing an audience, knowing somehow that the right person will claim their Purple Paper message—days, months, and even years later. Powered by my life's purpose and a fierce determination, a divine message manifests into an earthly gift.

Day after day, month after month, year after year, many thousands have been written, the majority copied, and all treasured securely in numerous binders. The original Purple Paper is divinely delivered to the one for whom the words were delicately transcribed from the voice of love. Thousands have made their way home, but many hundreds, some dated years ago, are safely held and honored daily until I come face-to-face, heart-to-heart, soul-to-soul with the one for whom it has been waiting.

Many Purple Papers have come and gone. Grace and love will continue to shine more brightly than light itself and bring further messages to those in need. It is not physically possible for me to hand deliver these powerfully charged messages of hope and love to everyone, which is why some yet undelivered messages are included in this book. My hope is that you or someone you know may find one of these messages and know, without question or doubt, that it is a sacred love letter written from the heavens especially for you. Here are some of the many Purple Papers patiently waiting to find their home.

If you believe one of these Purple Paper messages may be yours, contact me via my website at www.RolandComtois.net.

6-22-2013: We went together to heaven. Grandpa, I'm still your little guy. I love you … I know you watch me all the time. We watch over you. *Top of the page: Me, Dad, you.* (*Somebody fell off a boat and drowned.*) *Bottom corner: On the desk is where we are.* (*Possibly pictures.*)

5-10-2013: Mrs. Lafrancois is at peace. Tell them I know how hard you tried to help me. I'm not tired anymore. I love how you did so much for me.

Channeled Messages for the Soul
Roland M. Comtois
www.rolandcomtois.net

7-14-2013

(osteoblastoma)

I finally have no pain. You were so good never to leave me. I love you (Mom). I found so many angels……

7-14-2013: (osteoblastoma) I finally have no pain. You were so good never to leave me. I love you (Mom). I found so many angels …

3-27-2015

Roland M. Comtois - The Purple Papers
Channeled Messages for the Soul
www.blessingsbyroland.com

① I'm sorry that it came to this. I wasn't in my mind when I jumped off the bridge. I know I've been forgiven.

After I passed away I had to heal. My spirit is broken anymore.

3-27-2015: I'm sorry that it came to this. I wasn't in my mind when I jumped off the bridge. I know I've been forgiven. After I passed away, I had to heal. My spirit is not broken anymore. *Top of the page:* Cross. Rainbow.

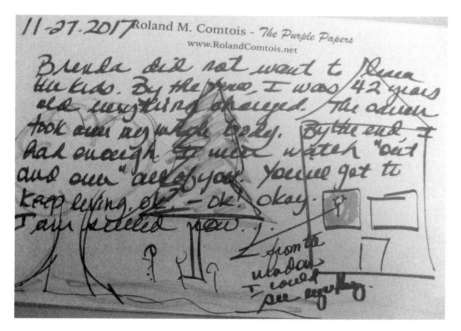

7-17-2014: Ray Jalette had very little pain. I tried to get things
cleared up, then I was gone. I'm sorry I left you with all the work.

11-27-2017: Brenda did not want to leave the kids. By the time I was 42 years old, everything
changed. The cancer took over my whole body. By the end, I had enough. I will watch "out
and over" all of you. You've got to keep living, OK?—OK! Okay. I am settled now. From the
window I could see everything. (*She is referring to seeing the kids playing in the yard.*)

12-12-2017: Jeanette found so much love in her life. I tried to be strong—because everyone needed me to be strong. I remember how hard you all worked on me in March. I couldn't breathe anymore. I couldn't really stay, but I did. You always made me happy. *Top of the page:* 4 mos.

6-5-2015: Mr. Gongeleski. (I found heaven even though no one will really believe it.) It's true that things happen fast, really fast.

12-12-2017: George wants to go back to the garage. I loved working on the cars. When my legs got funny, I couldn't do it anymore. I used to help everyone who needed assistance. Everyone came to see me. I loved it. I loved it all. About 6 weeks before I passed, I knew it was time. *Top of the page:* Junk too. Tools.

1-23-2018: Frank waited for everything to be right before he left. We all went through a lot when I was sick, especially your mother. I couldn't get my health back. After Christmas/holidays, I had nothing left in me. I waited and waited for the pain to go away. It didn't. It wasn't going to, so I passed on. Thanks for being around. *Top of the page:* Door to his room.

8-11-2013: Mom we are all together and it was not your fault.
I can see the water from the window and porch.

11-11-2014: Maria found Maria! Mother and daughter found each other (and Aunt Maria too.) Tell my family I was ready to let go of all the pain. I felt so much relief when I passed.

7-19-2016: Do you remember that lilac bush I planted when you were
a kid? It was so beautiful. I loved what you've done to honor me.
I'm so happy on the other side. Oh, yes, I found my "people."

11-21-2016: 1952. I had no choice, when I was young, working in the mill. I didn't like it, but
I needed to take care of you. I often wonder what if I took the other job. I'm sorry that we
couldn't be together for a long time. I'm sorry that you went through so much.

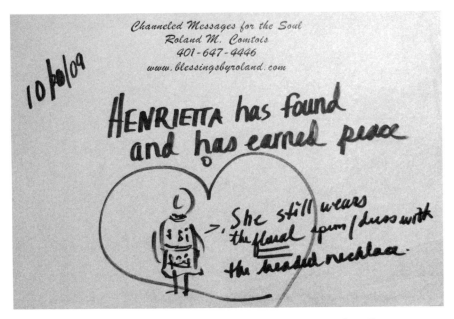

10-20-09: Henrietta has found and has earned peace. She still
wears the floral apron/dress with the beaded necklace.

10-7-2010: Harold found his true love. He waited for her
every day. I was there when she cried herself to sleep.

3-6-2018: Lloyd—I'm not here to tell my family I'm in heaven. They should know that already. I'm really wanting to tell my daughter that I made it my mission to watch over "the little girl." I did the first day you asked—years ago. And, yes, you are/have made the right decision about your own life.

5-15-2009: I was trying to fix something on the roof.

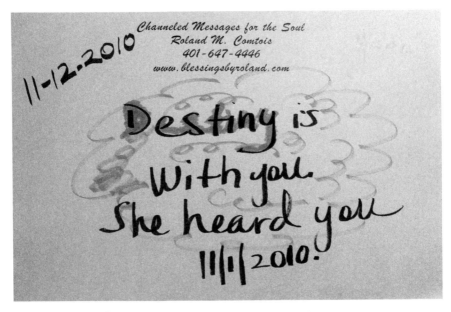

7-27-2010: Alma has found her healing love and peace.
My grandmother has the same name. I'm finally home.

11-12-2010: (*Baby*) Destiny is with you. She heard you 11/1/2010.

2-12-2012: (*September 11*) Tell Bonnie that I will always be there for her.
My voice is getting stronger (I called you). I know you believe it's me.
I watched over you for years so you could feel me there.

2-12-2012: I didn't know it would change like this. I am safe.
(*Playground. Three stars indicate nighttime.*)

10-5-2012: Tommy is free in heaven. He sits near you when you sit near the tree. I love you.

6-27-2017: Elizabeth and John have found each other again.
We were looking for each other for a little while (and there he was).
There is so much peace here—it's hard to believe. I/we are happy.

4-27-2018: Kevin—Tell my family to still have fun. Do you remember all the games we/I played? Go to the FIELD. It was a place I loved when I was a kid. We used to have so much fun there. And, my family, they are the best. I know I was young, but it's OK because I'm OK now. No pain.

6-4-2013: Baby Heather was carried by the angels to a place of love. When a butterfly comes, she sends a sign of HOPE. (*Two orange butterflies.*)

6-29-2016: Mia battled many things but not you. I came out of the treatments OK. It was 6 weeks later that it took hold of me. I was hoping that everything would clear up. I love you.
Top of the page: Sand dollars—shells—starfish (my favorite place).

6-29-2016: Jerry. I want you to know that I enjoyed our years of friendship. When we were young, we were good. I got in trouble near the end of my life. I became sick. I fought really hard to stay alive. I had help after I passed. (*Background drawing of two wedding bells.*)

Roland M. Comtois - *The Purple Papers*
Channeled Messages for the Soul
www.blessingsbyroland.com

6-29-2016: Do you remember "the dancing"? I remember everything about you. When we got married, you took care of me. And then, when I was getting sick, you did it again. I remember that beautiful red dress. Oh, how beautiful you are. I love you so much.

Roland M. Comtois - *The Purple Papers*
www.RolandComtois.net

9-8-2017: Theresa started to get sick a few days after her 69th birthday. "I spent a lot of time after that being very sick." I wanted to finally get peaceful, but it wasn't going to happen *here*. (Here being life.) I always believed in something—always—that helped me when I died.

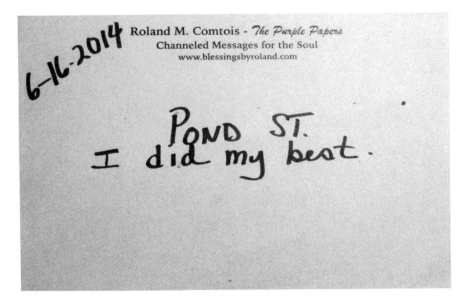

6-16-2014: Pond St. I did my best.

5-15-2014: Mr. Beauchemin was thinking about passing away. You know that all
I could do was stay in my room. I was tired of staying in my room. I am in heaven.

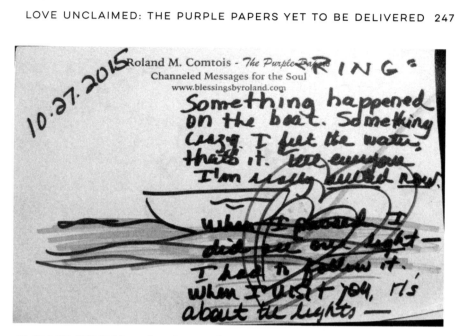

10-27-2015: "RING." Something happened on the boat. Something crazy. I felt the water, that's it. Tell everyone I'm really healed now. When I passed, I did see one light. I had to follow it. When I visit you, it's about the lights. (*The image has water and a boat.*)

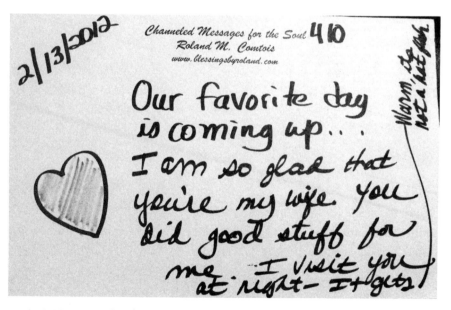

2-13-2012: 4-10. Our favorite day is coming up … I am so glad that you're my wife. You did good stuff for me. I visit you at night—it gets warm. It's not a hot flash.

5-8-2015: Raymond: Tell my family not to worry so much about me or where I am. I found two beautiful women. One being my mother (and the little girl). I know how hard you tried to heal my body. Now I am so happy.

TO WRITE TO THE AUTHOR

If you wish to contact the author or would like more information about this book, please write to the author in care of Llewellyn Worldwide Ltd. and we will forward your request. Both the author and publisher appreciate hearing from you and learning of your enjoyment of this book and how it has helped you. Llewellyn Worldwide Ltd. cannot guarantee that every letter written to the author can be answered, but all will be forwarded. Please write to:

Roland Comtois
℅ Llewellyn Worldwide
2143 Wooddale Drive
Woodbury, MN 55125-2989

Please enclose a self-addressed stamped envelope for reply,
or $1.00 to cover costs. If outside the U.S.A., enclose
an international postal reply coupon.

Many of Llewellyn's authors have websites with additional information and resources. For more information, please visit our website at http://www.llewellyn.com